1882 — Emma Jung — 1955

ANIMUS and ANIMA

By

EMMA JUNG

SPRING PUBLICATIONS, INC.
Dallas, Texas

Copyright 1957, 1981 by Spring Publications, Inc. All rights reserved
Copyright renewed 1985 by Spring Publications, Inc.

Published by Spring Publications, Inc.; Box 222069; Dallas, TX. 75222
Printed in the United States of America

Cover design and production by Maribeth Lipscomb and Patricia Mora

International Distributors:
Spring; Postfach; 8800 Thalwil; Switzerland
Japan Spring Sha, Inc.; 1–2–4, Nishisakaidani-Cho;
    Ohharano, Nishikyo-Ku; Kyoto, 610–11, Japan
Element Books Ltd; Longmead Industrial Estate;
    Shaftesbury, Dorset SP7 8PL; England

Library of Congress Cataloging-in-Publication Data

Jung, Emma.
    Animus ; and, Anima.

    Translation of : Ein Beitrag zum Problem des Animus,
and of : Anima.
    Originally published : New York : Analytical
Psychology Club of New York, 1957.
    1. Animus (Psychoanalysis) 2. Anima (Psychoanalysis)
I. Jung, Emma. Anima. English. 1985. II. Title.
BF175.5.A53J86   1985   150.19'54   85–18299
ISBN 0-88214-301-8

Eighth Printing 1987

CONTENTS

"On the Nature of the Animus" was read at the
Psychological Club of Zürich in November 1931
and was first published, in a slightly expanded
form, in *Wirklichkeit der Seele* (Zürich: Rascher
Verlag, 1934). The version read to the Club was
translated into English by Mrs. Baynes and appeared in *Spring 1941*. The present version has
been revised to correspond more closely with the
published German version. It is printed by permission of Rascher Verlag.

"The Anima as an Elemental Being" in German
was entitled "Die Anima als Naturwesen" and
appeared in *Studien zur analytischen Psychol-
ogie C. G. Jungs* (Zürich: Rascher Verlag,
1955), vol. 2. It is published here by permission
of the Curatorium of the C. G. Jung Institute,
Zürich.

The essays are reprinted with the additional permission of the Erbengemeinschaft Emma Jung.

ON THE NATURE

OF

THE ANIMUS

THE anima and the animus are two archetypal figures of especially great importance. They belong on the one hand to the individual consciousness and on the other hand are rooted in the collective unconscious, thus forming a connecting link or bridge between the personal and the impersonal, the conscious and the unconscious. It is because one is feminine and the other masculine that C. G. Jung has called them anima and animus respectively.[1] He understands these figures to be function complexes behaving in ways compensatory to the outer personality, that is, behaving as if they were inner personalities and exhibiting the characteristics which are lacking in the outer, and manifest, conscious personality. In a man, these are feminine characteristics, in a woman, masculine. Normally both are always present, to a certain degree, but find no place in the person's outwardly directed functioning because they disturb his outer adaptation, his established ideal image of himself.

However, the character of these figures is not determined only by the latent sexual characteristics they represent; it is conditioned by the experience each person has had in the course of his or her life with representatives of the other sex, and also by the collective image of woman carried in the psyche of the individual man, and the collective image of man carried by the woman. These three factors coalesce to form a quantity which is neither solely an image nor solely experience, but an entity not organically coordinated in its activity with the other psychic functions. It behaves as if it were a law unto itself, interfering in the life of the individual as if it were an alien element; sometimes the interference is helpful, sometimes disturbing, if not actually destructive. We have, therefore, every cause to concern ourselves with these psychic entities and arrive at an understanding of how they influence us.

If in what follows, I present the animus and its manifestations as realities, the reader must remember that I am speaking of psychic realities,[2] which are incommensurable with concrete realities but no less effective for that reason. Here I shall attempt to present certain aspects of the animus without, however, laying claim to a complete comprehension of this extraordinarily complex phenomenon. For in discussing the animus we are dealing not only with an absolute, an immutable entity, but also with a spiritual process. I intend to limit myself here to the ways in which the animus appears in its relation to the individual and to consciousness.

Conscious and Outward Manifestations of the Animus

The premise from which I start is that in the animus we are dealing with a masculine principle. But how is this masculine principle to be characterized? Goethe makes Faust, who is occupied with the translation of the Gospel of John, ask himself if the passage, "In the beginning was the Word," would not read better if it were, "In the beginning was Power," or

"Meaning," and finally he has him write, "In the beginning was the Deed." With these four expressions, which are meant to reproduce the Greek *logos,* the quintessence of the masculine principle does indeed seem to be expressed. At the same time, we find in them a progressive sequence, each stage having its representative in life as well as in the development of the animus. Power corresponds very well to the first stage, the deed follows, then the word, and finally, as the last stage, meaning. One might better say instead of power, directed power; that is will, because mere power is not yet human, nor is it spiritual. This four-sidedness characterizing the logos principle presupposes, as we see, an element of consciousness, because without consciousness neither will, word, deed, nor meaning is conceivable.

Just as there are men of outstanding physical power, men of deeds, men of words, and men of wisdom, so, too, does the animus image differ in accordance with the woman's particular stage of development or her natural gifts. This image may be transferred to a real man who comes by the animus role because of his resemblance to it; alternatively, it may appear as a dream or phantasy figure; but since it represents a living psychic reality, it lends a definite coloration from within the woman herself to all that she does. For the primitive woman, or the young woman, or for the primitive in every woman, a man distinguished by physical prowess becomes an animus figure. Typical examples are the heroes of legend, or present-day sports celebrities, cowboys, bull fighters, aviators, and so on. For more exacting women, the animus figure is a man who accomplishes deeds, in the sense that he directs his power toward something of great significance. The transitions here are usually not sharp, because power and deed mutually condition one another. A man who rules over the "word" or over "meaning" represents an essentially intellectual tendency, because word and meaning correspond par excellence to mental capacities. Such a man exemplifies the animus in the narrower sense, understood as being a spiritual guide and as representing the intellectual gifts of the woman. It is at this stage, too, for the most part, that the animus becomes problematical, hence, we shall have to dwell on it longest.

Animus images representing the stages of power and deed are projected upon a hero figure. But there are also women in whom this aspect of masculinity is already harmoniously coordinated with the feminine principle and lending it effective aid. These are the active, energetic, brave, and forceful women. But also there are those in whom the integration has failed, in whom masculine behavior has overrun and suppressed the feminine principle. These are the over-energetic, ruthless, brutal, men-women, the Xantippes who are not only active but aggressive. In many women, this primitive masculinity is also expressed in their erotic life, and then their approach to love has a masculine aggressive character and is not, as is usual in women, involved with and determined by feeling but functions on its own, apart from the rest of the personality, as happens predominantly with men.

On the whole, however, it can be assumed that the more primitive forms of masculinity have already been assimilated by women. Generally speaking, they have long ago found their applications in the feminine way of life, and there have long been women whose strength of will, purposefulness, activity, and energy serve as helpful forces in their otherwise quite feminine lives. The problem of the woman of today seems rather to lie in her attitude to the animus-logos, to the masculine-intellectual element in the narrower sense; because the extension of consciousness in general, greater consciousness in all fields, seems to be an inescapable demand — as well as a gift — of our time. One expression of this is the fact that along with the discoveries and inventions of the last fifty years, we have also had the beginning of the so-called woman's movement, the struggle of women for equal rights with men. Happily, we have today survived the worst product of this struggle, the "bluestocking." Woman has learned to see that she cannot become like a man because first and foremost she is a woman and must be one. However, the fact remains that a certain sum of masculine spirit has ripened in woman's consciousness and must find its place and effectiveness in her personality. To learn to know these factors, to coordinate them so that they can play their part in a meaningful way, is an important part of the animus problem.

From time to time we hear it said that there is no necessity for woman to occupy herself with spiritual or intellectual matters, that this is only an idiotic aping of man, or a competitive drive betokening megalomania. Although this is surely true in many cases, especially of the phenomena at the beginning of the woman's movement, nevertheless, as an explanation of the matter, it is not justified. Neither arrogance nor presumption drives us to the audacity of wanting to be like God — that is, like man; we are not like Eve of old, lured by the beauty of the fruit of the tree of knowledge, nor does the snake encourage us to enjoy it. No, there has come to us something like a command; we are confronted with the necessity of biting into this apple, whether we think it good to eat or not, confronted with the fact that the paradise of naturalness and unconsciousness, in which many of us would only too gladly tarry, is gone forever.

This, then, is how matters stand fundamentally, even if on the surface appearances may sometimes be otherwise. And because so significant a turning point is concerned, we must not be astonished at unsuccessful efforts, and grotesque exaggerations, nor allow ourselves to be daunted by them. If the problem is not faced, if woman does not meet adequately the demand for consciousness or intellectual activity, the animus becomes autonomous and negative, and works destructively on the individual herself and in her relations to other people. This fact can be explained as follows: if the possibility of spiritual functioning is not taken up by the conscious mind, the psychic energy intended for it falls into the unconscious, and there activates the archetype of the animus. Possessed of the energy that has flowed back into the unconscious, the animus figure becomes autonomous, so powerful, indeed, that it can overwhelm the conscious ego, and thus finally dominate the whole personality. I must add here that I start with the view that in the human being there is a certain basic idea to be fulfilled, just as, for instance, in an egg or a seed corn there is already contained the idea of the life destined to come from it. Therefore I speak of a sum of available psychic energy which is intended for spiritual functions, and ought to be applied to them. Expressed figuratively in terms of economics, the situation is like that dealt with in a household budget, or other enterprise of some sort where certain sums of money are provided for certain purposes. In addition, from time to time sums previously used in other ways will become available, either because they are no longer needed for those purposes or because they cannot otherwise be invested. In many respects, this is the case with the woman of today. In the first place, she seldom finds satisfaction in the established religion, especially if she is a Protestant. The church which once to a large extent filled her spiritual and intellectual needs no longer offers her this satisfaction. Formerly, the animus, together with its associated problems, could be transferred to the beyond (for to many women the Biblical Father-God meant a metaphysical, superhuman aspect of the animus image), and as long as spirituality could be thus convincingly expressed in the generally valid forms of religion, no conflict developed. Only now when this can no longer be achieved, does our problem arise.

A further reason for the existence of a problem regarding the disposal of psychic energy is that through the possibility of birth control a considerable sum of energy has been freed. It is doubtful whether woman herself can rightly estimate how large is this sum which was previously needed to maintain a constant state of readiness for her biological task.

A third cause lies in the achievements of technology that substitute new means for so many tasks to which woman previously applied her inventiveness and her creative spirit. Where she formerly blew up a hearth fire, and thus still accomplished the Promethean act, today she turns a gas plug or an electrical switch and has no inkling of what she sacrifices by these practical novelties, nor what consequences the loss entails. For everything not done in the traditional way will be done in a new way, and that is not altogether simple. There are many women who, when they have reached the place where they are confronted by intellectual demands, say, "I would rather have another child," in order to escape or at least to postpone the uncomfortable and disturbing demand. But sooner or later a woman must accommodate herself to meet it, for the biological demands naturally decrease progressively after the first half of life so that in any case a change of attitude is unavoidable, if she does not want to fall victim to a neurosis or some other form of illness.

Moreover, it is not only the freed psychic energy that confronts her with a new task, but equally the aforementioned law of the time-moment, the *kairos*, to which we are all subject and from which we cannot escape, obscure though its terms appear to us to be. In fact, our time seems quite generally to require a widening of consciousness. Thus, in psychology, we have discovered and are investigating the unconscious; in

physics, we have become aware of phenomena and processes —
rays and waves, for instance — which up till now were imperceptible and not part of our conscious knowledge. New worlds,
with the laws that govern them, open up as, for example, that
of the atom. Furthermore, telegraph, telephone, radio, and
technically perfected instruments of every sort bring remote
things near, expanding the range of our sense perceptions
over the whole earth and even far beyond it. In all of this, the
extension and illumination of consciousness is expressed. To
discuss further the causes and aims of this phenomenon would
lead us too far afield; I mention it only as a joint factor in the
problem which is so acute for the woman of today, the animus
problem.

The increase in consciousness implies a leading over of
psychic energy into new paths. All culture, as we know, de-
pends on such a deflection, and the capacity to bring it about
is what distinguishes men from animals. But this process involves great difficulties; indeed, it affects us almost like a sin,
a misdeed, as is shown in such myths as the Fall of man, or the
theft of fire by Prometheus, and that is how we may experience it in our own lives. Nor is this astonishing since it con-
cerns the interruption or reversal of the natural course of
events, a very dangerous venture. For this reason, this process
has always been closely connected with religious ideas and
rites. Indeed, the religious mystery, with its symbolical experience of death and rebirth, always means this mysterious and
miraculous process of transformation.

As is evident in the myths just mentioned concerning the
Fall of man and the stealing of fire by Prometheus, it is the
logos — that is, knowledge, consciousness, in a word — that
lifts man above nature. But this achievement brings him into
a tragic position between animal and God. Because of it, he
is no longer the child of mother nature; he is driven out of

paradise, but also, he is no god, because he is still tied inescapably to his body and its natural laws, just as Prometheus was fettered to the rock. Although this painful state of suspension, of being torn between spirit and nature, has long been familiar to man, it is only recently that woman has really begun to feel the conflict. And with this conflict, which goes hand in hand with an increase of consciousness, we come back to the animus problem that eventually leads to the opposites, to nature and spirit and their harmonization.

How do we experience this problem? How do we experience the spiritual principle? First of all, we become aware of it in the outside world. The child usually sees it in the father, or in a person taking the place of the father; later, perhaps, in a teacher or elder brother, husband, friend, finally, also, in the objective documents of the spirit, in church, state, and society with all their institutions, as well as in the creations of science and the arts. For the most part, direct access to these objective forms of the spirit is not possible for a woman; she finds it only through a man, who is her guide and intermediary. This guide and intermediary then becomes the bearer or representative of the animus image; in other words, the animus is projected upon him. As long as the projection succeeds, that is, as long as the image corresponds to a certain degree with the bearer, there is no real conflict. On the contrary, this state of affairs seems to be, in a certain sense, perfect, especially when the man who is the spiritual intermediary is also at the same time perceived as a human being to whom one has a positive, human relationship. If such a projection can be permanently established this might be called an ideal relationship, ideal because without conflict, but the woman remains unconscious. The fact that today it is no longer fitting to remain so unconscious seems, however, to be proved by the circumstance that many if not most women who believe themselves to be happy and content in what purports to be a perfect animus relationship are troubled with nervous or bodily symptoms. Very often anxiety states appear, sleeplessness and general nervousness, or physical ills such as headache and other pains, disturbances of vision, and, occasionally, lung affections. I know of several cases in which the lungs became affected at a time when the animus problem became acute, and were cured after the problem was recognized and understood as such.[3] (Perhaps the organs of breathing have a peculiar relationship to spirit, as is suggested by the words animus or pneuma and *Hauch,* breath, or *Geist,* spirit, and therefore react with special sensitivity to the processes of the spirit. Possibly any other organ could just as well be affected, and it is simply a question of psychic energy which, finding no suitable application and driven back upon itself, attacks any weak point.)

Such a total transference of the animus image as that described above creates, together with an apparent satisfaction and completeness, a kind of compulsive tie to the man in question and a dependence on him that often increases to the point of becoming unbearable. This state of being fascinated by another and wholly under his influence is well known under the term "transference," which is nothing else than projection. However, projection means not only the transference of an image to another person, but also of the activities that go with it, so that a man to whom the animus image has been transferred is expected to take over all the functions that have remained undeveloped in the woman in question, whether the thinking function, or the power to act, or responsibility toward the outside world. In turn, the woman upon whom a man has projected his anima must feel for him, or make relationships for him, and this symbiotic relationship is, in my opinion, the real cause for the compulsive dependence that exists in these cases.

But such a state of completely successful projection is usually not of very long duration — especially not if the woman is in a close relationship to the man in question. Then the incongruity between the image and the image-bearer often becomes all too obvious. An archetype, such as the animus represents, will never really coincide with an individual man, the less so the more individual that man is. Individuality is really the opposite of the archetype, for what is individual is not in any way typical but the unique intermixture of characteristics, possibly typical in themselves.

When this discrimination between the image and the person sets in we become aware, to our great confusion and disappointment, that the man who seemed to embody our image does not correspond to it in the least, but continually behaves quite differently from the way we think he should. At first we perhaps try to deceive ourselves about this and often succeed relatively easily, thanks to an aptitude for effacing differences, which we owe to blurred powers of discrimination. Oftentimes we try with real cunning to make the man be what we think he ought to represent. Not only do we consciously exert force or pressure; far more frequently we quite unconsciously force our partner, by our behavior, into archetypal or animus reactions. Naturally, the same holds good for the man in his attitude toward the woman. He, too, would like to see in her the image that floats before him, and by this wish, which works like a suggestion, he may bring it about that she does not live her real self but becomes an anima figure. This, and the fact that the anima and animus mutually constellate each other (since an anima manifestation calls forth the animus, and vice versa, producing a vicious circle very difficult to break), forms one of the worst complications in the relations between men and women.

But by the time the incongruity between the man and the

animus figure has been discovered, a woman is already in the midst of the conflict, and there remains nothing for her to do but to carry through to completion the process of discriminating between the image within and the man outside. Here we come to what is most essentially meaningful in the animus problem, namely, the masculine-intellectual component within the woman herself. It seems to me that to relate to this component, to know it, and to incorporate it into the rest of the personality, are central elements of this problem, which is perhaps the most important of all those concerning the woman of today. That the problem has to do with a natural predisposition, an organic factor belonging to the individuality and intended to function, explains why the animus is able to attract psychic energy to itself until it becomes an overwhelming and autonomous figure.

It is probable that all organs or organic tendencies attract to themselves a certain amount of energy, which means readiness for functioning, and that when a particular organ receives an insufficient amount of energy this fact is made known by the manifestation of disturbances or by the development of symptoms. Applying this idea to the psyche, I would conclude from the presence of a powerful animus figure — a so-called "possession by the animus" — that the person in question gives too little attention to her own masculine-intellectual logos tendency, and has either developed and applied it insufficiently or not in the right way. Perhaps this sounds paradoxical because, seen from the outside, it appears as if it were the feminine principle which is not taken sufficiently into account, since the behavior of such women seems on the surface to be too masculine and suggests a lack of femininity. But in the masculinity brought to view, I see more of a symptom, a sign that something masculine in the woman claims attention. It is true that what is primarily feminine is overrun and repressed by the autocratic entrance upon the scene of this masculinity, but the feminine element can only get into its right place by a detour that includes coming to terms with the masculine factor, the animus.

To busy ourselves simply in an intellectual or objectively masculine way seems insufficient, as can be seen in many women who have completed a course of study and practice a heretofore masculine, intellectual calling, but who, nonetheless, have never come to terms with the animus problem. Such a masculine training and way of life may well be achieved by identification with the animus, but then the feminine side is left out in the cold. What is really necessary is that feminine intellectuality, logos in the woman, should be so fitted into the nature and life of the woman that a harmonious cooperation between the feminine and masculine factors ensues and no part is condemned to a shadowy existence.

The first stage on the right road is, therefore, the withdrawal of the projection by recognizing it as such, and thus freeing it from the object. This first act of discrimination, simple as it may seem, nonetheless means a difficult achievement and often a painful renunciation. Through this withdrawal of the projection we recognize that we are not dealing with an entity outside ourselves but a quality within; and we see before us the task of learning to know the nature and effect of this factor, this "man in us," in order to distinguish him from ourselves. If this is not done, we are identical with the animus or possessed by it, a state that creates the most unwholesome effects. For when the feminine side is so overwhelmed and pushed into the background by the animus, there easily arise depressions, general dissatisfaction, and loss of interest in life. These are all intelligible symptoms pointing to the fact that one half of the personality is partly robbed of life by the encroachment of the animus.

Besides this, the animus can interpose itself in a disturbing way between oneself and other people, between oneself and life in general. It is very difficult to recognize such a possession in oneself, all the more difficult the more complete it is. Therefore it is a great help to observe the effect one has on other people, and to judge from their reactions whether these can possibly have been called forth by an unconscious animus identification. This orientation derived from other people is an invaluable aid in the laborious process — often beyond one's individual powers — of clearly distinguishing the animus and assigning it to its rightful place. Indeed, I think that without relationship to a person with respect to whom it is possible to orient oneself again and again, it is almost impossible ever to free oneself from the demonic clutch of the animus. In a state of identification with the animus, we think, say, or do something in the full conviction that it is we who are doing it, while in reality, without our having been aware of it, the animus has been speaking through us.

Often it is very difficult to realize that a thought or opinion has been dictated by the animus and is not one's own most particular conviction, because the animus has at its command a sort of aggressive authority and power of suggestion. It derives this authority from its connection with the universal mind, but the force of suggestion it exercises is due to woman's own passivity in thinking and her corresponding lack of critical ability. Such opinions or concepts, usually brought out with great aplomb, are especially characteristic of the animus. They are characteristic in that, corresponding to the principle of the logos, they are generally valid concepts or truths which, though they may be quite true in themselves, do not fit in the given instance because they fail to consider what is individual and specific in a situation. Ready-made, incontrovertibly valid judgments of this kind are really only applicable in mathematics, where two times two is always four. But in life they do not apply for there they do violence, either to the subject under discussion or to the person being addressed, or even to the woman herself who delivers a final judgment without having taken all of her own reactions into account.

The same sort of unrelated thinking also appears in a man when he is identified with reason or the logos principle and does not himself think, but lets "it" think. Such men are naturally especially well-suited to embody the animus of a woman. But I cannot go into this further because I am concerned here exclusively with feminine psychology.

One of the most important ways that the animus expresses itself, then, is in making judgments, and as it happens with judgments, so it is with thoughts in general. From within, they crowd upon the woman in already complete, irrefutable forms. Or, if they come from without, she adopts them because they seem to her somehow convincing or attractive. But usually she feels no urge to think through and thus really to understand the ideas which she adopts and, perhaps, even propagates further. Her undeveloped power of discrimination results in her meeting valuable and worthless ideas with the same enthusiasm or with the same respect, because anything suggestive of mind impresses her enormously and exerts an uncanny fascination upon her. This accounts for the success of so many swindlers who often achieve incomprehensible effects with a sort of pseudo-spirituality. On the other hand, her lack of discrimination has a good side; it makes the woman unprejudiced and therefore she frequently discovers and appraises spiritual values more quickly than a man, whose developed critical power tends to make him so distrustful and prejudiced that it often takes him considerable time to see a value which less prejudiced persons have long since recognized.

The real thinking of women (I refer here to women in general, knowing well that there are many far above this level who have already differentiated their thinking and their spiritual natures to a high degree) is preeminently practical and applied. It is something we describe as sound common sense, and is usually directed to what is close at hand and personal. To this extent it functions adequately in its own place and does not actually belong to what we mean by animus in the stricter sense. Only when woman's mental power is no longer applied to the mastering of daily tasks but goes beyond, seeking a new field of activity, does the animus come into play.

In general, it can be said that feminine mentality manifests an undeveloped, childlike, or primitive character; instead of the thirst for knowledge, curiosity; instead of judgment, prejudice; instead of thinking, imagination or dreaming; instead of will, wishing.

Where a man takes up objective problems, a woman contents herself with solving riddles; where he battles for knowledge and understanding, she contents herself with faith or superstition, or else she makes assumptions. Clearly, these are well-marked pre-stages that can be shown to exist in the minds of children as well as in those of primitives. Thus, the curiosity of children and primitives is familiar to us, as are also the roles played by belief and superstition. In the *Edda* there is a riddle-contest between the wandering Odin and his host, a memorial of the time when the masculine mind was occupied with riddle-guessing as woman's mind is still today. Similar stories have come down to us from antiquity and the Middle Ages. We have the riddle of the Sphinx, or of Oedipus, the hair-splitting of the sophists and scholastics.

So-called wishful thinking also corresponds to a definite stage in the development of the mind. It appears as a motif in fairy tales, often characterizing something in the past, as when the stories refer to "the time when wishing was still helpful." The magic practice of wishing that something would befall a person is founded on the same idea. Grimm, in his German mythology, points to the connection between wishing, imagining, and thinking. According to him,

"An ancient Norse name for Wotan or Odin seems to be Oski or Wish, and the Valkyries were also called Wish Maidens. Odin, the wind-god and wanderer, the lord of the army of spirits, the inventor of runes, is a typical spirit god, but of a primitive form still near to nature."

As such, he is lord of wishes. He is not only the giver of all that is good and perfect as comprehended under wishing, but also it is he who, when evoked, can create by a wish. Grimm says, "Wishing is the measuring, outpouring, giving, creating power. It is the power that shapes, imagines, thinks, and is therefore imagination, idea, form." And in another place he writes: "In Sanskrit 'wish' is significantly called *manoratha,* the wheel of the mind — it is the wish that turns the wheel of thought."

The woman's animus in its superhuman, divine aspect is comparable to such a spirit and wind-god. We find the animus in a similar form in dreams and phantasies, and this wish-character is peculiar to feminine thinking. If we bear in mind that power to imagine means to man nothing less than the power to make at will a mental image of anything he chooses, and that this image, though immaterial, cannot be denied reality, then we can understand how it is that imagining, thinking, wishing, and creating have been rated as equivalents. Especially in a relatively unconscious condition, where outer and inner reality are not sharply distinguished but flow into one another, it is easily possible that a spiritual reality, that is, a thought or an image, can be taken as concretely real. In primitives, too, there is to be found this equivalence between outer concrete and inner spiritual reality. (Lévy-Bruhl[4] gives many examples of this, but it would take us too far afield to say more about it here.) The same phenomenon is found very clearly expressed in feminine mentality.

We are astonished to discover, on closer inspection, how often the thought comes to us that things must happen in a certain way, or that a person who interests us is doing this or that, or has done it, or will do it. We do not pause to compare these intuitions with reality. We are already convinced of their truth, or at least are inclined to assume that the mere idea is true and that it corresponds to reality. Other phantasy structures also are readily taken as real and can at times even appear in concrete form.

One of the animus activities most difficult to see through lies in this field, namely, the building up of a wish-image of one-self. The animus is expert at sketching in and making plausible a picture that represents us as we would like to be seen, for example, as the "ideal lover," the "appealing, helpless child," the "selfless handmaiden," the "extraordinarily original person," the "one who is really born to something better," and so on. This activity naturally lends the animus power over us until we voluntarily, or perforce, make up our minds to sacrifice the highly colored picture and see ourselves as we really are.

Very frequently, feminine activity also expresses itself in what is largely a restrospectively oriented pondering over what we ought to have done differently in life, and how we ought to have done it; or, as if under compulsion, we make up strings of causal connections. We like to call this thinking; though, on the contrary, it is a form of mental activity that is strangely pointless and unproductive, a form that really leads only to self-torture. Here, too, there is again a characteristic failure to discriminate between what is real and what has been thought or imagined.

We could say, then, that feminine thinking, in so far as it is not occupied practically as sound common sense, is really not thinking, but, rather, dreaming, imagining, wishing, and fearing (i.e., negative wishing). The power and authority of the animus phenomenon can be partly explained by the primitive mental lack of differentiation between imagination and reality. Since what belongs to mind — that is, thought — possesses at the same time the character of indisputable reality, what the animus says seems also to be indisputably true.

And now we come to the magic of words. A word, also, just like an idea, a thought, has the effect of reality upon undifferentiated minds. Our Biblical myth of creation, for instance, where the world grows out of the spoken word of the Creator, is an expression of this. The animus, too, possesses the magic power of words, and therefore men who have the gift of oratory can exert a compulsive power on women in both a good and an evil sense. Am I going too far when I say that the magic of the word, the art of speaking, is the thing in a man through which a woman is most unfailingly caught and most frequently deluded? But it is not woman alone who is under the spell of word-magic, the phenomenon is prevalent everywhere. The holy runes of ancient times, Indian *mantras,* prayers, and magic formulas of all sorts down to the technical expressions and slogans of our own times, all bear witness to the magic power of spirit that has become word.

However, it can be said in general that a woman is more susceptible to such magic spells than a man of a corresponding cultural level. A man has by nature the urge to understand the things he has to deal with; small boys show a predilection for pulling their toys to pieces to find out what they look like inside or how they work. In a woman, this urge is much less pronounced. She can easily work with instruments or machines without its ever occurring to her to want to study or understand their construction. Similarly, she can be impressed by a significant-sounding word without having grasped its exact meaning. A man is much more inclined to track down the meaning.

The most characteristic manifestation of the animus is not in a configured image (*Gestalt*) but rather in words (*logos* also means word). It comes to us as a voice commenting on every situation in which we find ourselves, or imparting generally applicable rules of behavior. Often this is how we first perceive the animus to be different from the ego, long before it has crystallized into a personal figure. As far as I have observed, this voice expresses itself chiefly in two ways. First, we hear from it a critical, usually negative comment on every movement, an exact examination of all motives and intentions, which naturally always causes feelings of inferiority, and tends to nip in the bud all initiative and every wish for self-expression. From time to time, this same voice may also dispense exaggerated praise, and the result of these extremes of judgment is that one oscillates to and fro between the consciousness of complete futility and a blown-up sense of one's own value and importance. The animus' second way of speaking is confined more or less exclusively to issuing commands or prohibitions, and to pronouncing generally accepted viewpoints.

It seems to me that two important sides of the logos function are expressed here. On the one hand, we have discriminating, judging, and understanding; on the other, the abstracting and setting up of general laws. We could say, perhaps, that where the first sort of functioning prevails the animus figure appears as a single person, while if the second prevails, it appears as a plurality, a kind of council. Discrimination and judgment are mainly individual, while the setting up and abstracting of laws presupposes an agreement on the part of many, and is therefore more appropriately expressed by a group.

It is well known that a really creative faculty of mind is a rare thing in woman. There are many women who have developed their powers of thinking, discrimination, and criticism to a high degree, but there are very few who are mentally creative in the way a man is. It is maliciously said that woman is so lacking in the gift of invention, that if the kitchen spoon had not been invented by a man, we would today still be stirring the soup with a stick!

The creativity of woman finds its expression in the sphere of living, not only in her biological functions as mother but in the shaping of life generally, be it in her activity as educator, in her role as companion to man, as mother in the home, or in some other form. The development of relationships is of primary importance in the shaping of life, and this is the real field of feminine creative power. Among the arts, the drama is outstandingly the one in which woman can achieve equality with man. In acting, people, relationships, and life are given form, and so woman is there just as creative as man. We come upon creative elements also in the products of the unconscious, in the dreams, phantasies, or phrases that come spontaneously to women. These products often contain thoughts, views, truths, of a purely objective, absolutely impersonal nature. The mediation of such knowledge and such contents is essentially the function of the higher animus.

In dreams we often find quite abstract scientific symbols which are hardly to be interpreted personally but represent objective findings or ideas at which no one is more astonished, perhaps, than the dreamer herself. This is especially striking in women who have a poorly developed thinking function or a limited amount of culture. I know a woman in whom thinking is the "inferior function,"[5] whose dreams often mention problems of astronomy and physics, and also refer to technical instruments of all sorts. Another woman, quite nonrational in type, when reproducing unconscious contents, drew strictly geometric figures, crystal-like structures, such as are found in text books on geometry or mineralogy. To others still, the animus brings views of the world and of life that go far beyond their conscious thinking and show a creative quality that cannot be denied.

However, in the field where the creative activity of woman flowers most characteristically, that is, in human relationships, the creative factor springs from feeling coupled with intuition or sensation, more than from mind in the sense of logos. Here, the animus can be actually dangerous, because it injects itself into the relationship in place of feeling, thus making relatedness difficult or impossible. It happens only too frequently that instead of understanding a situation — or another person — through feeling and acting accordingly, we think something about the situation or the person and offer an opinion in place of a human reaction. This may be quite correct, well-intentioned, and clever, but it has no effect, or the wrong effect, because it is right only in an objective, factual way. Subjectively, humanly speaking, it is wrong because in that moment the partner, or the relationship, is best served not by discernment or objectivity but by sympathetic feeling. It very often happens that such an objective attitude is assumed by a woman in the belief that she is behaving admirably, but the effect is to ruin the situation completely. The inability to realize that discernment, reasonableness, and objectivity are inappropriate in certain places is often astonishing. I can only explain this by the fact that women are accustomed to think of the masculine way as something in itself more valuable than the feminine way and superior to it. We believe a masculine objective attitude to be better in every case than a feminine and personal one. This is especially true of women who have already attained a certain level of consciousness and an appreciation of rational values.

Here I come to a very importance difference between the animus problem of the woman and the anima problem of the man, a difference which seems to me to have met with too little attention. When a man discovers his anima and has come to terms with it, he has to take up something which previously seemed inferior to him. It counts for little that naturally the anima figure, be it image or human, is fascinatingly attractive and hence appears valuable. Up to now in our world, the feminine principle, as compared to the masculine, has always stood for something inferior. We only begin at present to render it justice. Revealing expressions are, "only a girl," or, "a boy doesn't do that," as is often said to boys to suggest that their behavior is contemptible. Then, too, our laws show clearly how widely the concept of woman's inferiority has prevailed. Even now in many places the law frankly sets the man above the woman, gives him greater privileges, makes him her guardian, and so on. As a result, when a man enters into relationship with his anima he has to descend from a height, to overcome a resistance — that is, his pride — by acknowledging that she is the "Sovereign Lady" (*Herrin*) as Spitteler called her, or, in Rider Haggard's words, "She-who-must-be-obeyed."

With a woman the case is different. We do not refer to the animus as "He-who-must-be-obeyed," but rather as the opposite, because it is far too easy for the woman to obey the authority of the animus — or the man — in slavish servility. Even though she may think otherwise consciously, the idea that what is masculine is in itself more valuable than what is feminine is born in her blood. This does much to enhance the power of the animus. What we women have to overcome in our relation to the animus is not pride but lack of self-confidence and the resistance of inertia. For us, it is not as though we had to demean ourselves (unless we have been identified with the animus), but as if we had to lift ourselves. In this, we often fail for lack of courage and strength of will. It seems to us a presumption to oppose our own unauthoritative conviction to those judgments of the animus, or the man, which claim a general validity. For a woman to work herself up to a point of such apparently presumptuous spiritual independence often costs a great deal, especially because it can so easily be mis-understood or misjudged. But without this sort of revolt, no matter what she has to suffer as a consequence, she will never be free from the power of the tyrant, never come to find her-self. Viewed from the outside, it often seems to be just the other way round; because all too frequently one is aware only of an overweening assurance and aplomb, and very little modesty or lack of confidence is evident. In reality, this defiant and self-assured, or even contentious attitude, should be di-rected against the animus, and is so intended at times, but generally it is the sign of a more or less complete identification with it.

Not only in Europe do we suffer from this now superannu-ated veneration of men, this overvaluation of the masculine. In America, too, where it is customary to speak of a cult of woman, the attitude does not seem to be fundamentally differ-ent. An American woman physician of wide experience has told me that all her women patients suffer from a depreciation of their own sex, and that with all of them she has to drive home the necessity of giving the feminine its due value. On the other hand, there are extremely few men who undervalue their own sex; they are, on the contrary, for the most part extremely proud of it. There are many girls who would gladly be men, but a youth or man who would like to be a girl would be looked upon as almost perverse.

The natural result of this situation is that a woman's posi-tion with respect to her animus is quite different from a man's relation to his anima. And because of this difference in atti-tude, many phenomena which the man cannot understand as parallel to his anima experience, and vice versa, are to be ascribed to the fact that in these problems the task of the man and the woman are different.

To be sure, the woman does not escape sacrifice. Indeed, for her to become conscious means the giving up of her specifically feminine power. For by her unconsciousness, woman exerts a magical influence on man, a charm that lends her power over him. Because she feels this power instinctively and does not wish to lose it, she often resists to the utmost the process of becoming conscious, even though what belongs to the spirit may seem to her extremely worth striving for. Many women even keep themselves artificially unconscious solely to avoid making this sacrifice. It must be admitted that the woman is very often backed up in this by the man. Many men take pleasure in woman's unconsciousness. They are bent on opposing her development of greater consciousness in every possible way, because it seems to them uncomfortable and unnecessary.

Another point which is often overlooked and which I would like to mention lies in the function of the animus in contrast to that of the anima. We usually say offhand that animus and anima are the mediators between the unconscious contents and consciousness, meaning by this that both do exactly the same thing. This is indeed true in a general way, but it seems important to me to point out the difference in the roles played by the animus and the anima. The transmission of the unconscious contents in the sense of making them visible is the special role of the anima. It helps the man to perceive these otherwise obscure things. A necessary condition for this is a sort of dimming of consciousness; that is, the establishment of a more feminine consciousness, less sharp and clear than man's, but one which is thus able to perceive in a wider field things that are still shadowy. Woman's gift as seer, her intuitive faculty, has always been recognized. Not having her vision brought to a focus gives her an awareness of what is obscure and the power to see what is hidden from a keener eye. This vision, this perception of what is otherwise invisible, is made possible for the man by the anima.

With the animus, the emphasis does not lie on mere perception — which as was said has always been woman's gift — but true to the nature of the logos, the stress is on knowledge, and especially on understanding. It is the function of the animus to give the meaning rather than the image.

It would be a mistake to think that we are making use of the animus if we turn ourselves over to passive phantasies. We must not forget that as a rule it is no achievement for a woman to give rein to her powers of phantasy; non-rational happenings or images whose meaning is not understood seem something quite natural to her; while to the man, occupation with these things is an achievement, a sort of sacrifice of reason, a descent from the light into darkness, from the clear into the turbid. Only with difficulty does he say to himself that all the incomprehensible or even apparently senseless contents of the unconscious may, nonetheless, have a value. Moreover, the passive attitude which visions demand accords little with the active nature of a man. To a woman, this does not seem difficult; she has no reservations against the non-rational, no need to find at once a meaning in everything, no disinclination to remaining passive while things sweep over her. For women to whom the unconscious is not easily accessible, who only find entrance to its contents with difficulty, the animus can become more of a hindrance than a help if it tries to understand and analyze every image that comes up before it can be properly perceived. Only after these contents have entered consciousness and perhaps already taken form ought the animus to exert its special influence. Then, indeed, its aid is invaluable, because it helps us to understand and to find a meaning.

Yet sometimes a meaning is communicated to us directly from the unconscious, not through images or symbols, but through flashes of knowledge already formulated in words. This, indeed, is a very characteristic form of expression of the animus. Yet it is often difficult to discover whether we are dealing with a familiar, generally valid, and hence collective opinion, or with the result of individual insight. In order to be clear about this, conscious judgment is again needed, as well as exact discrimination between oneself and the animus.

The Animus as it Appears in the Images of the Unconscious

Having tried to show in the foregoing how the animus manifests itself outwardly and in consciousness, I would like now to discuss how the images of the unconscious represent it, and how it appears in dreams and phantasies. Learning to recognize this figure and holding occasional conversations and debates with it are further important steps on our way to discriminating between ourselves and the animus. The recognition of the animus as an image or figure within the psyche marks the beginning of a new difficulty. This is due to its manifoldness. We hear from men that the anima almost always appears in quite definite forms which are more or less the same in all men; it is mother or loved one, sister or daughter, mistress or slave, priestess or witch; upon occasion it appears with contrasting characteristics, light and dark, helpful and destructive, now as a noble, and now as an ignoble being.

On the contrary, for women the animus appears either as a plurality of men, as a group of fathers, a council, a court, or some other gathering of wise men, or else as a lightning-change artist who can assume any form and makes extensive use of this ability.

I explain this difference in the following way: Man has really experienced woman only as mother, loved one, and so on, that is, always in ways related to himself. These are the forms in which woman has presented herself, the forms in which her fate has always been carried out. The life of man, on the contrary, has taken on more manifold forms, because his biological task has allowed him time for many other activities. Corresponding to the more diversified field of man's activity, the animus can appear as a representative or master of any sort of ability or knowledge. The anima figure, however, is characterized by the fact that all of its forms are at the same time forms of relationship. Even if the anima appears as priestess or witch, the figure is always in a special relationship to the man whose anima it embodies, so that it either initiates or bewitches him. We are again reminded of Rider Haggard's *She,* where the special relationship is even represented as being centuries old.

But as has been said, the animus figure does not necessarily express a relationship. Corresponding to the factual orientation of man and characteristic of the logos principle, this figure can come on the scene in a purely objective, unrelated way, as sage, judge, artist, aviator, mechanic, and so on. Not infrequently it appears as a "stranger." Perhaps this form in particular is the most characteristic, because, to the purely feminine mind, the spirit stands for what is strange and unknown.

The ability to assume different forms seems to be a characteristic quality of spirit; like mobility, the power to traverse great distances in a short time, it is expressive of a quality which thought shares with light. This is connected with the wish-form of thinking already mentioned. Therefore, the animus often appears as an aviator, chauffeur, skier, or dancer, when lightness and swiftness are to be emphasized. Both of these characteristics, transmutability and speed, are found in many myths and fairy tales as attributes of gods or magicians. Wotan, the wind-god and leader of the army of spirits, has already been mentioned; Loki, the flaming one, and Mercury, with the winged heels, also represent this aspect of the logos, its living, moving, immaterial quality which, without fixed qualities, is to a certain extent only a dynamism expressing the possibility of form, the spirit, as it were, that "bloweth where it listeth."

In dreams or phantasies, the animus appears chiefly in the figure of a real man: as father, lover, brother, teacher, judge, sage; as sorcerer, artist, philosopher, scholar, builder, monk (especially as a Jesuit); or as a trader, aviator, chauffeur, and so forth; in short, as a man distinguished in some way by mental capacities or other masculine qualities. In a positive sense, he can be a benevolent father, a fascinating lover, an understanding friend, a superior guide; or, on the other hand, he can be a violent and ruthless tyrant, a cruel task-master, moralist and censor, a seducer and exploiter, and often, also, a pseudo-hero who fascinates by a mixture of intellectual brilliance and moral irresponsibility. Sometimes he is represented by a boy, a son or a young friend, especially when the woman's own masculine component is thus indicated as being in a state of becoming. In many women, as I have said, the animus has a predilection for appearing in a plural form as a council which passes judgment on everything that is happening, issues precepts or prohibitions, or announces generally accepted ideas.[6] Whether it appears most often as one person with a changing mask or as many persons at the same time may depend on the natural gifts of the woman in question, or on the phase of her development at the moment.

I cannot enter here into all the manifold, personal, phenomenal forms of the animus, and therefore content myself with a series of dreams and phantasies which show how it presents itself to the inner eye, how it appears in the light of the dream-world. These are examples in which the archetypal character of the animus figures is especially clear, and which at the same time point to a development. The figures in this series of dreams appeared to the woman concerned at a time when independent mental activity had become a problem, and the animus image had begun to detach itself from the person upon whom it had been projected.

There appeared then in a dream a bird-headed monster whose body was just a distended sac or bladder able to take on any and every form. This monster was said to have been formerly in possession of the man upon whom the animus was projected, and the woman was warned to protect herself against it because it liked to devour people, and if this happened, the person was not killed outright but had to continue living inside the monster.

The bladder form pointed to something still in an initial stage — only the head, the characteristic organ for an animus, was differentiated. It was the head of a creature of the air; for the rest, any shape could arise. The voracity indicated that a need for extension and development existed in this still undifferentiated entity. The attribute of greediness is illuminated by a passage from the *Khandogya Upanishad*,[7] which deals with the nature of Brahma. It is said there:

"The wind is in truth the All-Devourer, for when the fire dies out it goes into the wind, when the sun sets, it goes into the wind, when the moon sets, it goes into the wind, when the waters dry up, they go into the wind, for the wind consumes them all. Thus it is with respect to the divinity. And now with respect to the self. The breath is in truth the All-Devourer, for when a man sleeps, speech goes into breath, the eye goes into breath, the ear too, and the *manas*, for the breath consumes them all. These then are the two All-Devourers; wind among the gods, and breath among living men."

Together with this bird-headed creature of the air there appeared to the woman a sort of fire spirit, an elementary being consisting only of flame and in perpetual motion, calling himself the son of the "lower mother." Such a mother figure, in contrast to a heavenly, light mother, embodies the primordial feminine as a power that is heavy, dark, earth-bound, a power versed in magic, now helpful, now witch-like and uncanny, and often actually destructive. Her son, then, would be a chthonic fire-spirit, recalling Logi or Loki of northern mythology, who is represented as a giant endowed with creative power and at the same time as a sly, seductive rascal, later on the prototype of our familiar devil. In Greek mythology, Hephaestus, god of the fire of the earth, corresponds to him, but Hephaestus in his activity as smith points to a controlled fire, while the northern Loki incorporates a more elementary, undirected force of nature. This earth fire-spirit, the son of the lower mother, is close to woman and familiar to her. He expresses himself positively in practical activity, particularly in the handling of material and in its artistic treatment. He is expressed negatively in states of tension or explosions of affect, and often, in a dubious and calamitous way, he acts as confederate to the primordial feminine in us, becoming the instigator or auxiliary force in what are generally termed "feminine devils' or witches' arts." He could be characterized as a lower or inferior logos, in contrast to a higher form which appeared as the bird-headed air creature and which corresponds to the wind-and-spirit-god, Wotan, or to the Hermes who leads souls to Hades. Neither of these, however, is born of the lower mother, both belong only to a faraway, heavenly father.

The motif of the variable form returned again in the following dream where a picture was shown bearing the title, "Urgo, the Magic Dragon."

A snake or dragon-like creature was represented in the picture together with a girl who was under his power. The dragon had the ability to stretch out in all directions so that there was no possibility for the girl to evade his reach; at any movement of hers he could extend himself on that side and make escape impossible.

The girl, who can be taken as the soul, somewhat in the sense of the unconscious individuality, is a constantly recurring figure in all these dreams and phantasies. In our dream-picture she had only a shadowy outline, with blurred features. Still entirely in the power of the dragon, each of her movements was observed and measured by him, so that her escape seemed impossible.

However, development is shown in the following phantasy, placed in India:

A magician is having one of his dancers perform before the king. Hypnotized by magic, the girl dances a dance of transformations, in which, throwing off one veil after another, she impersonates a motley succession of figures, both animals and men. But now, despite the fact that she has been hypnotized by the magician, a mysterious influence is exerted upon her by the king. She goes more and more into ecstasy. Disregarding the order of the magician to stop, she dances on and on, till finally, as though throwing off her body like a last veil, she falls to the earth, a skeleton. The remains are buried; out of the grave a flower grows, out of the flower, in turn, a white woman.

Here we have the same motif, a young girl in the power of a magician whose commands have to be obeyed without choice. But in the figure of the king, the magician has an opponent who sets a limit to the magician's power over the girl and brings it about that she no longer dances at command but of her own volition. The transformation, previously only indicated, now becomes a reality, because the dancer dies and then comes up from the earth in a changed and purified form.

The doubling of the animus figure here is especially important; on the one hand, he appears as the magician, on the other, as the king. In the magician, the lower form of the animus representing magic power is represented; it makes the girl take on or imitate various roles, while the king, as already said, embodies the higher principle which brings about a real transformation, not just a representation of one. An important function of the higher, that is, the personal animus, is that as a true psychopompos it initiates and accompanies the soul's transformation.

A further variation of this theme is given in the same dream: the girl has a ghostly lover who lives in the moon, and who comes regularly in the shallop of the new moon to receive a blood sacrifice which she has to make to him. In the interval, the girl lives in freedom among people as a human being. But at the approach of the new moon, the spirit turns her into a rapacious beast and, obeying an irresistible force, she has to climb a lonely height, and bring her lover the sacrifice. This sacrifice, however, transforms the moon-spirit, so that he himself becomes a sacrificial vessel, which consumes itself but is again renewed, and the smoking blood is turned into a plant-like form out of which spring many-colored leaves and flowers.

In other words, by the blood received, that is, by the psychic energy given to it, the spiritual principle loses its dangerously compulsive and destructive character and receives an independent life, an activity of its own.

The same principle appears as Bluebeard, a well-known form of animus handed down to us in story form. Bluebeard seduces women and destroys them in a secret way and for equally secret purposes.

In our case, he bears the appropriate name of Amandus. He lures the girl into his house, gives her wine to drink, and afterwards takes her into an underground chamber to kill her. As he prepares himself for this, a sort of intoxication overcomes the girl. In a sudden impulse of love, she embraces the murderer, who is immediately robbed of his power and dissolves in air, after promising to stand by her side in the future as a helpful spirit.

Just as the ghostly spell of the moon-bridegroom was broken by the blood sacrifice — by the giving of psychic energy — so here, by embracing the terrifying monster, the girl destroys his power through love.

In these phantasies I see indications of an important archetypal form of the animus for which there are also mythological parallels, as, for example, in the myth and cult of Dionysus. The ecstatic inspiration which seized the dancer in our first phantasy and which overcame the girl in the story of Bluebeard-Amandus is a phenomenon characteristic of the Dionysian cult. There also it is chiefly women who serve the god and become filled with his spirit. Roscher[8] emphasizes the fact that this service of Dionysus by women is contrary to the otherwise general custom of having the gods attended by persons of their own sex.

In the story of the moon-spirit, the blood sacrifice and transformation of the girl into an animal are themes for which parallels can also be found in the cult of Dionysus. There, living animals were sacrificed or torn to pieces by the raving maenads in their wild and god-inflicted madness. The Dionysian celebrations also differed from the cults of the Olympic gods in that they took place at night on the mountains and in the forests, just as in our phantasy the blood-offering to the moon-spirit took place at night on a mountain top. Some familiar figures from literature come to mind in this connection, as, for instance, the Flying Dutchman, the Pied Piper or Rat Catcher of Hamelin, and the Water Man or Elfin King of folk songs, all of whom employ music to lure maidens into their water- or forest-kingdoms. The "Stranger" in Ibsen's *Lady from the Sea* is another such figure in a modern setting.

Let us consider more closely the Rat Catcher as a characteristic form of the animus. The tale of the Rat Catcher is familiar: he lured the rats from every crack and corner with his piping; they had to follow him, and not only the rats, but also the children of the city — which had refused to reward his services — were irresistibly drawn after him and made to disappear into his mountain. One is reminded of Orpheus who could elicit such magic sounds from his lyre that men and beasts were forced to follow him. This feeling of being irresistibly lured and led away into unknown distances of waters, forests, and mountains, or even into the underworld, is a typical animus phenomenon, it seems to me, and difficult to explain because, contrary to the other activities of the animus, it does not lead to consciousness but to unconsciousness, as these disappearances into nature or the underworld show. Odin's Thorn of Sleep, which sent any person it touched into a deep slumber, is a similar phenomenon.

The same theme is very tellingly formulated in Sir James M. Barrie's play, *Mary Rose*. Mary Rose, who has accompanied her husband on a fishing expedition, is supposed to be waiting for him on a small island called "The Island-That-Wants-To-Be-Visited." But while she waits, she hears her name called; she follows the voice and vanishes completely. Only after a lapse of many years does she reappear, still exactly as she was at the time of her disappearance, and she is convinced that she has been on the island only a few hours, in spite of all the years that have intervened.

What is depicted here as vanishing into nature or the underworld, or as a prick from the Thorn of Sleep, is experienced by us in ordinary living when our psychic energy withdraws from consciousness and from all application to life, disappearing into some other world, we know not where. When this happens, the world into which we go is a more or less conscious phantasy or fairy land, where everything is either as we wish it to be or else fitted out in some other way to compensate the outer world. Often these worlds are so distant and lie at such depths that no recollection of them ever penetrates our waking consciousness. We notice, perhaps, that we have been drawn away somewhere but we do not know where, and even when we return to ourselves we cannot say what took place in the interval.

To characterize more closely the form of the spirit which is acting in these phenomena, we might compare its effects to those of music. The attraction and abduction is often, as in the tale of the Rat Catcher, effected by music. For music can be understood as an objectification of the spirit; it does not express knowledge in the usual logical, intellectual sense, nor does it shape matter; instead, it gives sensuous representation to our deepest associations and most immutable laws. In this sense, music is spirit, spirit leading into obscure distances beyond the reach of consciousness; its content can hardly be grasped with words — but strange to say, more easily with numbers — although simultaneously, and before all else, with feeling and sensation. Apparently paradoxical facts like these show that music admits us to the depths where spirit and nature are still one — or have again become one. For this reason, music constitutes one of the most important and primordial forms in which woman ever experiences spirit. Hence also the important part which music and the dance play as means of expression for women. The ritual dance is clearly based on spiritual contents.

This abduction by the spirit to cosmic-musical regions, remote from the world of consciousness, forms a counterpart to the conscious mentality of women, which is usually directed only toward very immediate and personal things. Such an experience of abduction, however, is by no means harmless or unambiguous. On the one hand, it may be no more than a lapse into unconsciousness, a sinking away into a sort of sleeping twilight state, a slipping back into nature, equivalent to regressing to a former level of consciousness, and therefore useless, even dangerous. On the other hand it may mean a genuine religious experience and then, of course, it is of the highest value.

Along with the figures already mentioned, which show the animus in a mysterious, dangerous aspect, there stands another figure of a different sort. In the case we are discussing, it is a star-headed god, guarding in his hand a blue bird, the bird of the soul. This function of guarding the soul belongs, like that of guiding it, to the higher supra-personal form of the animus. This higher animus does not allow itself to change into a function subordinate to consciousness, but remains a superior entity and wishes to be recognized and respected as such. In the Indian phantasy about the dancer, this higher, masculine spiritual principle is embodied in the figure of the king; thus, he is a commander, not in the sense of a magician but in the sense of a superior spirit having nothing of the earth or the night about him. He is not a son of the lower mother, but an ambassador of a distant, unknown father, a supra-personal power of light.

All these figures have the character of archetypes[9] — hence the mythological parallels — as such they are correspondingly impersonal, or supra-personal, even though on one side they are turned toward the individual and related to her. Appearing with them is the personal animus that belongs to her as an individual; that is, the masculine or spiritual element which corresponds to her natural gifts and can be developed into a

conscious function or attitude, coordinated with the totality
of her personality. It appears in dreams as a man with whom
the dreamer is united, either by ties of feeling or blood, or by
a common activity. Here are to be found again the forms of
the upper and lower animus, sometimes recognizable by positive and negative signs. Sometimes it is a long-sought friend
or brother, sometimes a teacher who instructs her, a priest who
practices a ritual dance with her, or a painter who will paint
her portrait. Then again, a workman named "Ernest" comes to
live in her house, and an elevator boy, "Constantin," takes
service with her. Upon other occasions, she has to struggle
with an impudent rebellious youth, or she must be careful
of a sinister Jesuit, or she is offered all sorts of wonderful things
by Mephistophelian tradesmen. A distinctive figure, though
appearing only rarely, is that of the "stranger." Usually this
unknown being, familiar to her in spite of his strangeness,
brings, as an ambassador, some message or command from the
distant Prince of Light.

With the passage of time, figures such as these described
here become familiar shapes, as is the case in the outer world
with people to whom one is close or whom one meets often.
One learns to understand why now this figure, now that appears. One can talk to them, and ask them for advice or help,
yet often there is occasion to guard oneself against their insist-
ence, or to be irritated at their insubordination. And the
attention must always be alert to prevent one or another of
these forms of the animus from arrogating supremacy to itself
and dominating the personality. To discriminate between oneself and the animus, and sharply to limit its sphere of power,
is extraordinarily important; only by doing so is it possible
to free oneself from the fateful consequences of identifying
with the animus and being possessed by it. Hand in hand with
this discrimination goes the growth of consciousness and the

realization of the true Self, which now becomes the decisive factor.

In so far as the animus is a supra-personal entity, that is, a spirit common to all women, it can be related to the individual woman as a soul guide and helpful genius, but it cannot be subordinated to her conscious mind. The situation is different with the personal entity which wishes to be assimilated, with the animus as brother, friend, son, or servant. Confronted with one of these aspects of the animus, the woman's task is to create a place for it in her life and personality, and to initiate some undertaking with the energy belonging to it. Usually our talents, hobbies and so on, have already given us hints as to the direction in which this energy can become active. Often, too, dreams point the way, and in keeping with the individual's natural bent, mention will be made in them of studies, books, and definite lines of work, or of artistic or executive activities. But the undertakings suggested will always be of an objective practical sort corresponding to the masculine entity which the animus represents. The attitude demanded here — which is, to do something for its own sake and not for the sake of another human being — runs counter to feminine nature and often can be achieved only with effort. But this attitude is just what is important, because otherwise the demand that is part of the nature of the animus, and therefore justified, will obtrude itself in other ways, making claims which are not only inappropriate, as has already been said, but which produce precisely the wrong effects.

Apart from these specific activities, the animus can and should help us to gain knowledge and a more impersonal and reasonable way of looking at things. For the woman, with her automatic and oftentimes altogether too subjective sympathy, such an achievement is valuable; it can even be an aid in the field most peculiarly her own, that of relationship. For example, her own masculine component can help her to understand a man — and this should be emphasized — for even though the automatically functioning animus, with its inappropriate "objectivity," does have a disturbing effect on human relationships, nonetheless, it is also important for the development and good of the relationship that the woman should be able to take an objective, impersonal attitude.

Thus we see that there are not only intellectual activities in which animus power can work itself out, but that above all it makes possible the development of a spiritual attitude which sets us free from the limitation and imprisonment of a narrowly personal standpoint. And what comfort and help it gives us to be able to raise ourselves out of our personal troubles to supra-personal thoughts and feelings, which, by comparison, make our misfortunes seem trivial and unimportant!

To attain such an attitude and to be able to fulfil the appointed task, requires, above everything else, discipline, and this bears harder on woman, who is still nearer to nature, than on man. Unquestionably, the animus is a spirit which does not allow itself to be hitched to a wagon like a tame horse. Its character is far too much that of the elemental being; for our animus may lag leadenly behind us in a lethargy, or confuse us with unruly, flickering inspirations, or even soar entirely away with us into thin air. Strict and unfailing guidance is needed to control this unstable directionless spirit, to force it to obey and to work toward a goal.

For a large number of women today, however, the way is different. I refer to those who through study or some other artistic, executive, or professional activity, have accustomed themselves to discipline before they became aware of the animus problem as such. For these, if they have sufficient talent, identification with the animus is entirely possible.

However, as far as I have been able to observe, the problem of how to be a woman frequently arises in the midst of the most successful professional activity. Usually it appears in the form of dissatisfaction, as a need of personal, not merely objective values, a need for nature, and femininity in general. Very often, too, the problem arises because these women, without wanting to, become entangled in difficult relationships; or, by accident or fate, they stumble into typically feminine situations toward which they do not know what attitude to take. Then their dilemma is similar to that of the man with respect to the anima; that is, these women, too, are confronted with the difficulty of sacrificing what, to a certain degree, is a higher human development, or at least a superiority. They have to accept what is regarded as less valuable, what is weak, passive, subjective, illogical, bound to nature — in a word, femininity.

But in the long run both these different ways presuppose the same goal, and whichever way we go, the dangers and difficulties are the same. Those women for whom intellectual development and objective activity are only of secondary importance are also in danger of being devoured by the animus, that is, of becoming identical with it. Therefore it is of the greatest importance that we have a counterpoise which can hold the forces of the unconscious in check and keep the ego connected with the earth and with life.

First and foremost, we find such a check in increasing consciousness and the ever firmer feeling of our own individuality; secondly, in work in which the mental powers can be applied; and last but not least, in relationships to other people which establish a human bulwark and orientation point, over against the supra- or non-human character of the animus. The relationship of a woman to other women has great meaning in this connection. I have had occasion to observe that as the animus problem became acute, many women began to show an increased interest in other women, the relationship to women being felt as an ever-growing need, even a necessity. Perhaps this may be the beginning of a feminine solidarity, heretofore wanting, which becomes possible now only through our growing awareness of a danger threatening us all. Learning to cherish and emphasize feminine values is the primary condition of our holding our own against the masculine principle which is mighty in a double sense — both within the psyche and without. If it attains sole mastery, it threatens that field of woman which is most peculiarly her own, the field in which she can achieve what is most real to her and what she does best — indeed, it endangers her very life.

But when women succeed in maintaining themselves against the animus, instead of allowing themselves to be devoured by it, then it ceases to be only a danger and becomes a creative power. We women need this power, for, strange as it seems, only when this masculine entity becomes an integrated part of the soul and carries on its proper function there is it possible for a woman to be truly a woman in the higher sense, and, at the same time, also being herself, to fulfil her individual human destiny.

NOTES

1. C. G. Jung. *Psychological Types*. New York: Harcourt, Brace & Co., Inc., 1926. Chap. XI, sects. 48, 49; also "The Relations Between the Ego and the Unconscious" in *Two Essays on Analytical Psychology*. Bollingen Series XX. New York: Pantheon Press, 1953. Pt. II, Chap. II.
2. Concerning the concept of psychic reality, see the works of C. G. Jung, especially *Psychological Types, l.c.*, Chap. I.

3. See M. Esther Harding. *The Way of All Women*. New York: Long-
    mans, Green & Co., 1933.
4. Lucien Lévy-Bruhl. *Primitive Mentality*. London: G. Allen & Unwin
    Ltd., 1923, and *The Soul of the Primitive*. New York: The Macmillan
    Co., 1928.
5. C. G. Jung. *Psychological Types. l.c.,* Chap. XI, sect. 30.
6. Excellent examples of animus figures are to be found in fiction, see
    Ronald Fraser. *The Flying Draper*. London: Jonathan Cape, 1924;
    also *Rose Anstey*. London: Jonathan Cape, 1930; Marie Hay. *The
    Evil Vineyard*. Leipzig: Tauchnitz, 1924; Théodore Flournoy. *From
    India to the Planet Mars*. Translated by D. B. Vermilye. New York:
    Harper Bros., 1900.
7. "Khandogya" in *The Upanishads*. Translated by F. Max Mueller.
    Oxford: Clarendon Press, 1900, p. 58.
8. See W. J. Roscher. *Lexikon der griechischen und römischen Mytho-
    logie,* under *"Dionysus."*
9. C. G. Jung. *Psychological Types. l.c.,* Chap. XI, sect. 26; also *Two
    Essays. l.c.,* p. 135.

THE ANIMA

AS AN ELEMENTAL BEING

THE concept of elemental beings dwelling in water and air, in earth and fire, in animals and plants, is age-old and occurs all over the world, as is shown by countless examples in mythology and fairy tales, folklore and poetry. Because these concepts reveal an astounding similarity not only to each other, but also to figures in the dreams and phantasies of modern people, we are led to conclude that more or less constant factors must underlie them, factors which always and everywhere express themselves in similar ways.

The researches of depth psychology have shown that the images and figures produced by the spontaneous, myth-making faculty of the psyche are not to be understood as merely reproducing or paraphrasing outer phenomena. They are also expressions of inner psychic facts and may therefore be regarded as one kind of psychic self-representation. This point of view can also be applied to the ideas of elemental beings, and in what follows we shall inquire whether and in what ways the anima is reflected in them. A comprehensive survey of the material is impossible here. I can give only a few examples, and, in connection with them, discuss only the characteristics which seem to me to be important in my context. That is why, among all the elemental creatures, the giants, dwarves, elves, and so on, I am considering solely those which, because of their female sex or their relation to a man, can be accounted embodiments of the anima. For the anima, as is well known, represents the feminine personality components of the man and at the same time the image which he has of feminine nature in general, in other words, the archetype of the feminine.

Therefore, these figures cannot be considered anima figures unless they contain typical and clearly recognizable feminine traits, and we shall give special attention to such traits in the hope of gaining a profounder insight into the nature of the anima generally. Among the beings in question the best suited for such an investigation are the nymphs, swan maidens, undines, and fairies, familiar from so many legends and tales. As a rule, they are of enticing beauty but only half human; they have fish tails, like the nixie, or turn into birds, like the swan maidens. Often they appear as more than one, especially as three; the undifferentiated animus also likes to appear as more than one.

With charms or enchanting songs these beings (sirens, the Lorelei, and so on) lure a man into their realm, where he disappears forevermore; or else — a very important point — they try to bind the man in love, that they may live in his world with him. Always they have something uncanny about them, and there is a taboo connected with them that must not be broken.

The figure of the swan maiden is exceedingly ancient and can almost be called mythological. She comes from very far back and appears all over the world. Probably the earliest literary formulation of this motif is the story of Purûravas and Urvasî, which is found in one of the oldest Vedic writings, the *Rig-Veda*,[1] and more clearly and in more detail in the *Satapatha-Brahmana*.[2] I will give the latter version in a somewhat shortened form.

Urvasî the nymph *(apsara)*³ loved Purûravas and agreed to marry him upon her own conditions. She said: "Thrice a day shalt thou embrace me but do not lie with me against my will and let me not see thee naked, for such is the way to behave to us women."

After living with him for several years she became pregnant, and the Gandharvas,³ finding that she had lingered long enough among human beings, devised a means for her return. A ewe with two lambs, had been tied to her couch; these they stole during the night, one after the other, and each time she cried out: "Alas, they are taking away my darling, as if where is no hero and no man!"

Hearing this, Purûravas sprang up, naked as he was, to follow the robbers, and at that instant the Gandharvas produced a flash of lightning so that Urvasî beheld her husband "as by daylight." Thus one of her conditions had been broken and so, when Purûravas returned, she had vanished.

In despair he wandered about the country, hoping to find Urvasî again, and one day he came to a lotus lake on which "there were nymphs swimming about it in the shape of swans," and she whom he sought was among them. When she saw Purûravas, she showed herself in human form, and recognizing her, he pleaded: "Oh, my wife, stay thou, cruel in mind: let us now exchange words! Untold, these secrets of ours will not bring us joy . . ."

She replied: "What concern have I with speaking to thee? I have passed away like the first of the dawns. Purûravas, go home again: I am like the wind difficult to catch . . ."

Sorrowing, he said: "Then will thy friend rush away this day never to come back, to go to the farthest distance . . ." (to the wolf-infested wilderness).

She replied: "Purûravas, do not die! do not rush away! let not the cruel wolves devour thee! Truly, there is no friendship with women, and their hearts are the hearts of hyenas . . ." She added that, while among mortals, she had eaten a little sacrificial fat every day and still felt sated with it.

But finally her heart took pity on him and she told him to come back in a year. Then his son would have been born and then, too, she would lie with him for one night. When he came on the last night of the year, lo, there stood a golden palace, and he was told to enter it, and his wife was brought to him. The next morning the Gandharvas offered him a boon and when, upon Urvasî's advice, he asked to become one of them, they granted his wish. But first he had to offer a sacrifice, and the Gandharvas put fire into a bowl and gave it to him for the purpose. He took the fire and the son who had been born to him back to his native village. Then, after seeking out suitable sticks for the sacrificial fire, he lighted them in the way that the Gandharvas had prescribed, and became a Gandharva himself.

This ancient legend, early as it is, shows the typical features which we find in later versions and in other localities. For example, union with such a being involves a definite set of conditions, non-fulfilment of which will be fatal. In our tale, for instance, Purûravas may not be seen naked by Urvasî. A similar prohibition occurs in the famous story of "Cupid and Psyche,"[4] only there it is reversed, in that Psyche is forbidden the sight of her divine husband, whereas Urvasî does not want to see the human Purûravas naked, that is, does not want to see his reality. Even though the breaking of this command is unintentional, it results in the nymph's return to her element. When she says that she is sated with the bits of sacrificial fat which she consumed during her sojourn with Purûravas, this also seems to indicate that human reality is not to her taste; moreover, when she returns to her own world she draws her husband after her. To be sure, a son is mentioned to whom she gives birth after her disappearance and whom Purûravas brings home later, so that apparently something with a place in the human realm results from their union, but one learns nothing further about it.[5]

In this relation the attitudes of Purûravas and the heavenly nymph are markedly different; he, with human feeling, laments the loss of his beloved, he tries to find her again and wants to speak with her, but her words, when she says that women have the hearts of hyenas, are the expression of a soul-less elemental being passing judgment on itself.

As to the interpretation of swan maidens, the school which conceived of mythological images as embodiments of natural forces and events saw in them the mist which floats above the water and then, arising, condenses into clouds and moves across the sky like swans flying. Even from the psychological point of view the comparison of these figures with mist and clouds is apt, for apparently as long as what are called the unconscious contents remain unconscious, or almost so, they are without firm outlines and can change, turn into each other, and transform themselves. Only when they emerge from the unconscious and are grasped by consciousness do they become plainly and clearly recognizable, and only then can anything definite be said about them. Really one does better not to picture the unconscious as an actual area, with firmly defined, quasi-concrete contents; such a concept is only occasionally helpful when it serves to bring the imperceptible closer to our understanding. In hypnagogic visions or representations of unconscious contents a cloudlike formation often appears at the initial stage of a development which takes definite shape later. Something of the kind floated before Goethe's vision when he allowed Mephisto to say, in describing the realm of the Mothers to Faust:

> ". . . . . Escape from the Existent
> To phantoms' unbound realms far distant!
> Delight in what long since exists no more!
> Like filmly clouds the phantoms glide along.
> Brandish the key, hold off the shadowy throng."[6]

From this we may conclude that the femininity represented by the nymph, Urvasî, is as yet much too nebulous and incorporeal to live permanently and realize itself in the human realm, that is, in waking consciousness. Her words, "I have passed away like the first of the dawns . . . I am like the wind difficult to catch," also indicate the insubstantial, breathlike character of her being, conforming to that of a nature spirit and producing an impression of dreamlike unreality.

Entirely similar in character is "The Dream of Oenghus," an Irish legend ascribed to the eighth century.[7]

Oenghus, who was himself of mythical descent, saw in a dream a beautiful girl approaching his couch, but as he went to take her hand she sprang away from him. The following night the girl came again, this time with a lute in her hand, "the sweetest that ever was," and she played a tune to him. So it went on for an entire year and Oenghus fell into a "wasting sickness." But a physician diagnosed his trouble and thereupon messengers were sent to scour the whole of Ireland for the girl who — so the physician said — was destined to be his. Finally they discovered that her father was the king of a fairy hill and that she changed her shape into that of a swan every other year. To meet her, Oenghus must come on a definite day to a certain lake. Arriving there, he saw three times fifty swans upon the water, linked together in pairs by silver chains. But Oenghus called his dream lover by name, and she recognized him and said she would come ashore if he would promise that she might return to the lake again. When he promised, she came to him and he threw his arms about her. Then "they fell asleep in the form of two swans and went round the lake three times so that his promise might not be broken." Finally, as two white birds, they flew away (to his father's castle) and sang a beautiful choral song that put the people to sleep for three days and three nights. "The girl stayed with him after that."

The dreamlike character of this story is particularly clear. That Oenghus' still-unknown beloved appears to him first in a dream, that she is expressly said to be destined for him, and that he cannot live without her, are circumstances which unquestionably point to the anima — to his other half. He wins her by accepting her condition, and allowing her for a time at least to return to the water; indeed, he becomes a swan himself. In other words, he attempts to meet her in her own element, her *niveau,* in order to make her permanently his —

conduct which should also prove of value psychologically, in relating to the anima. The magical song of the two swans is an expression of the fact that two beings of opposite nature, who yet belong together, have now in harmonious concord been united.

The Nordic Valkyries are archaic and mythical swan maidens of quite a different sort. They are called Valkyries because, in the service of Odin, they recover the warriors fallen in battle and bear them to Valhalla.[8] They also have a role in bestowing victory and defeat, which shows plainly that they are related to the Norns, who spin and cut the threads of fate. On the other hand, when the Valkyrie in Valhalla hands the hero his drinking horn, she is performing the usual function of a serving maid. Yet offering a drink is a meaningful gesture, too, expressing relationship and a mutual tie; and certainly a motif which occurs frequently is that of the anima figure filling a man's cup with a potion of love, inspiration, transformation, or death. The Valkyries are also called Wish-Maidens,[9] and now and then one of them becomes, as Brünnehilde did, the wife or lover of a great hero to whom she gives help and protection in battle.

One may well see in these semi-divine creatures an archetypal form of the anima, to be expected in savage and war-loving men. Indeed it is said of the Valkyries that their principal passion is combat. They embody simultaneously, as is also the case with the anima, both the man's desire and his endeavor, and insomuch as these are directed towards battle, his feminine side appears in a form that is warlike. Furthermore, although the Valkyries are usually thought of as riding, they are also able to "course through air and water," and take the shape of swans.[10]

One of the oldest songs of the *Edda*, "the Song of Wayland,"[11] begins with the swan maiden motif:

"The maidens flew from the south
By the murky forest,
Young swan maidens,
Battle to waken.
There on the borders of the lake
They reposed awhile.
These southern maidens,
And spun fine flax."[12]

The song does not say, but allows us to guess that here, as in other similar stories, Wayland and his brothers stole the maids' swan garments so that they could not go away. Then each of the brothers took one of the maidens and

"They remained after
Seven winters
Dwelling there eight
In all affection;
But in the ninth,
Necessitated by duty
The maidens desired
To go to the murky forest,
Young swan maidens,
Battle to waken."

So they flew away, and two of the brothers followed to seek where they had vanished, but Wayland, fashioning gold rings, stayed at home and awaited their return.

There is nothing more about this in the further course of the song, which proceeds along another line.

The significant thing here is that the maidens feel an overwhelming yearning for battle and, by flying away, draw the brothers after them. In psychological language, this means that the yearning, the desire for new undertakings, makes itself felt first in the unconscious-feminine. Before coming clearly to consciousness, the striving for something new and different usually expresses itself in the form of an emotional stirring, a vague impulse or unexplainable mood. When this is given expression, as in "The Song of Wayland" and many other legends, through a feminine being, it means that the unconscious stirrings are transmitted to consciousness through the feminine element in the man, through his anima.

This occurrence starts an impulse, or acts like an intuition, disclosing new possibilities to the man and leading him on to pursue and grasp them. When the swan maiden wishes to incite to battle, she plays the anima's characteristic role of *femme inspiratrice* — although, to be sure, on a primitive level where the "work" to which the man is inspired is mainly that of fighting.

This is also a favorite role for women in the court poetry of the Middle Ages, albeit in a more refined form. The knight fights for his lady in a tournament, wearing her token — her sleeve, for instance — on his helmet; her presence fires him and raises his courage; she bestows the guerdon of victory upon him and frequently this consists of her love. But often she is cruel, demanding senseless and superhuman feats of her knight as the sign of his subservience.[13]

Count William IX of Poitiers, renowned as the first troubadour, is reported to have had the portrait of his beloved painted on his shield. However, in the literature of the troubadours, it is particularly interesting to see how the inspiration moved gradually to other things than fighting.

The name Lady Adventure *(Frau Adventiure)* is another evidence of the masculine love of adventure being personified in feminine form.

A further peculiarity of the swan maiden is that she foretells the future.[14] The Valkyries, in spinning the fortunes of battle[15] and so preparing the fate to be, resemble the Norns. And in turn, the latter, whose names are Wurd, Werdandi and Skuld,[16] appear to embody the natural life processes of becoming and passing away.

In the Celtic realm the same character is ascribed to the fairies, whose name is connected with *fatum*,[17] and who also like to appear in threes. Often it happens that the good bestowed by the first two is cancelled by the third, a feature likewise reminiscent of the Norns, or the Parcae.

The *Nibelungenlied*[18] relates that on their journey to King Etzel the Nibelungs came to the high waters of the Danube, and Hagen went ahead to look for a way across. There he heard water splashing and coming nearer saw *"wîsiu wîp"* (wise women) bathing in a beautiful spring. Creeping up, he took their garments and hid them. But if he would give them back, one of the women promised to tell him what would happen on the journey.

> "They floated like sea birds   before him on the flood.
> It seemed to him their foresight   must needs be sure and good.
> Whatever they should tell him   he therefore would believe."[19]

So here, too, wise women, resembling water birds, appear as foretellers of future events.

It is well known that the Germanic peoples ascribed to woman the gift of prophecy, and for this reason she was especially esteemed by them, even honored. Odin himself goes to a seeress, the Vala, to hear his fate. Tacitus[20] mentions a prophetess named Veleda, who enjoyed great authority among her clan, the Bructeri, and was brought to Rome as a captive in Vespasian's time, and Julius Caesar recounts that among the Germans it was customary "for the mothers of families to foretell, by casting lots and prophesying, whether it would be advisable to engage in battle or not . . ."[21]

Among the Greeks and Romans this function was exercised

by Pythia and the sibyls. And such concepts seem to have been preserved for a long time, as is shown by a story concerning Charlemagne, which Grimm reports[22] from a Leyden manuscript of the thirteenth century. The legend is intended to explain the name of Aachen, originally Aquisgranum, and says that:

> Charlemagne kept a wise woman there, "an enchantress or fairy, who by other names was also called a nymph, goddess, or dryad;"[23] with her he had intercourse, and she was alive while he remained with her but died when he went forth. One day, as he had his pleasure with her, he saw (that there was) a golden grain upon her tongue. He had it cut away, whereupon the nymph died and never came to life again.

This nymph recalls the mysterious Aelia Laelia Crispis discussed by C. G. Jung in "The Bologna Enigma."[24]

If we ask ourselves why second sight and the art of prophecy are ascribed to woman, the answer is that in general she is more open to the unconscious than man. Receptivity is a feminine attitude, presupposing openness and emptiness, wherefore Jung[25] has termed it the great secret of femininity. Moreover, the feminine mentality is less averse to irrationality than the rationally oriented masculine consciousness, which tends to reject everything not conforming to reason and so frequently shuts itself off from the unconscious. In the *Phaedrus* Plato criticizes this over-reasonable attitude — especially in the matter of love — and praises the irrational, even the insane, insofar as it may be a divine gift. He mentions several forms of this:

1. The oracular wisdom pronounced by the Pythia, for instance, when giving advice as to the welfare of the state. Concerning this he remarks: "For . . . the prophetess at Delphi and the priestesses of Dodona, when out of their senses, have conferred great benefits on Hellas, both in public and in private life, but when in their senses, few or none."[26]

2. The sibyl's gift of prophecy which foretells the future.

3. The frenzy *(enthousiasmos)* inspired by the Muses.

Pythia, the sibyls and the Muses are feminine beings and may be likened to the northern seeresses; their sayings are of an irrational kind that looks like madness from the standpoint of reason or the logos. Faculties such as these, however, do not belong to woman only; there have always been masculine seers and prophets, too, who are such by virtue of a feminine, receptive attitude which makes them responsive to influences from the other side of consciousness.

Because the anima, as the feminine aspect of man, possesses this receptivity and absence of prejudice toward the irrational, she is designated the mediator between consciousness and the unconscious. In the creative man, especially, this feminine attitude plays an important role; it is not without cause that we speak of the conception of a work, of carrying out a thought, delivering oneself of it, or brooding over it.

The swan maiden motif occurs also in countless fairy tales;[27] the story of "The Huntsman and the Swan Maiden" will serve as an example:

A forester, on the track of a deer, reached a lake just as three white swans came flying up. They immediately turned into three fair maidens who bathed themselves in the lake, but after a while they emerged from the water and flew away as swans. He could not get these maidens out of his mind and resolved to marry one of them. So three days later he returned to the lake and again found them bathing. Softly he crept up and took the swan mantle left on the shore by the youngest. She implored him to give it back to her but he pretended to be deaf and took it home, so that the maid had to follow after. She was received in friendly fashion by his people, and agreed to marry the hunter. But the swan mantle he gave to his mother who put it away in a chest. One day, after this pair had lived happily together for several years, the mother in tidying up found the little chest and opened it. As soon as the young woman caught sight of her swan mantle she threw it hurriedly around her, and with the words, "Who wants to see me again must come to the glass mountain that stands on the shining field"[28] she swung herself into the air and flew away. The unhappy hunter went to seek her and, with the assistance of friendly animals, after many difficulties, finally found her; then, having learned that she was enchanted, he set her free.

I have told this story in a good deal of detail because it includes a new and very significant motif, that of redemption. The need for redemption, shown by the enchantment, indicates that the swan form is not an original condition, but secondary, like a dress hiding the princess. Behind the animal form is concealed a higher being which must be redeemed and with which the hero will eventually unite.

The princess to be redeemed, appearing in so many fairy tales, clearly points to the anima. Since, however, the story shows that the princess was there before the swan, this surely hints at an original state of unity and wholeness, which was ended by the enchantment, and must now be recreated. The idea that a primal condition of perfection was destroyed, by either the sinful attitude of men or the envy of the gods, is a very ancient concept, forming the basis of many religious and philosophic systems. Evidences of this are the Biblical doctrine of man's fall, Plato's originally spherical primal being which split into halves, and the Gnostic Sophia imprisoned in matter.

In psychological terms we say that life's demands and the increasing development of consciousness destroy or mar the original wholeness of the child. For example, in the development of masculine ego-consciousness the feminine side is left behind and so remains in a "natural state." The same thing happens in the differentiation of the psychological functions;

the so-called inferior function remains behind and, as a result, is undifferentiated and unconscious. Therefore in the man it is usually connected with the likewise unconscious anima. Redemption is achieved by recognizing and integrating these unknown elements of the soul.

The fairy tale of "The Stolen Veil"[29] presents this theme in a new way characteristic of the Romantic period. Localized in the so-called Schwanenfeld[30] in the mountains of Saxony, where there is said to be a hidden, beauty-bestowing spring, the story contains the typical features already mentioned. Instead of her swan raiment, however, a veil (and ring) are stolen from the bather.

The hero, who is a knight, takes her to his home, where their wedding is to be celebrated; and in this tale, too, confides the care of the veil to his mother. Then, on the wedding day, the bride laments that she does not have it and the mother brings it to her; whereupon the bride, putting on the veil and a crown, immediately turns into a swan and flies out of the window.

This story is too long to give in detail. It should be noted, however, that the mother, apparently with good intentions, is again the one who gives back the bride's swan garment and so causes her departure.

Since the separation of the pair is brought about by the mother's action, it is possible to deduce a hidden rivalry between the mother and the anima, such as is often met with in actuality. On the other hand, this feature could also be understood as the tendency of the "Great Mother," that is, of the unconscious, to recall those who belong to her.

The swan maiden's royal descent, shown by her crown, marks her as a being of a higher order, and can be related to the superhuman, divine aspect of the anima. Yet in many stories it seems as if the figure of the enchanted princess should be interpreted from the standpoint of feminine psychology; in this case, she represents the woman's higher personality, her Self.[31] As for the bird shape: being a creature of the air, the bird symbolizes not only the animal quality of the natural being, but also contains an intimation of its unawakened spiritual potentialities.

Another elemental being enjoying special popularity and longevity is the nixie; theme of fairy tales, legends, and folksongs in every period, she is a figure made familiar to us by countless representations. Also, she serves as a subject for modern poets,[32] and often appears in dreams.

An ancient term, particularly favored by the poets of the thirteenth century for such watery beings, is *"Merminne,"*[33] or *"Merfei."* Because they possess, like the swan maidens, the gift of prophecy and a knowledge of natural things, they are also called *"wîsiu wîp"* (wise women). But in general, as we shall see, other factors take precedence over these, above all, the eros factor. This is shown by the movement known as *Frauendienst* or *Minnedienst,* which expressed the new attitude toward women and toward eros arising during the twelfth and thirteenth centuries and constituted a knightly counterpart to the nurture of logos values in the monasteries. As the poetry of the period shows, not least among the causes contributing to this higher evaluation of women was the clearer emergence and increased effectiveness of the anima.[34]

Being essentially feminine, the anima, like the woman, is predominantly conditioned by eros, that is, by the principle of union, of relationship, while the man is in general more bound to reason, to logos, the discriminating and regulative principle.

So the *Merminne* and their companions always have a love relationship to a man, or try to bring one about — an endeavor which is, indeed, a fundamental feminine aim. In this regard they differ from the swan maidens, who for the most part do not seek such a relationship of their own accord but, by the theft of their feather garments, fall into the man's power through a ruse. Hence they try to escape at the first opportunity. Such relationships are predominantly instinctive and lack psychological motive or any meaning beyond the instinctual. For a man to take possession of a woman more or less by force is a clear sign that his erotic attitude is at a completely primitive level. So it is not unreasonable for an elemental creature, upon uniting with such a man, to ask that she be done no violence, never be struck by his hand, or spoken to harshly.

Legends of water fairies and nixies are particularly widespread, especially in regions with a Celtic population. In many places these tales are connected with definite localities and families, particularly in Wales, Scotland and Ireland, where they have been current up until very recent times.

As one example among many I shall give a legend from Wales, recorded by John Rhys,[35] a well-known collector and student of Celtic folklore.

The events described are supposed to have occurred toward the end of the twelfth century in a village in Carmarthenshire in Wales. Here lived a widow with her son. One day, while pasturing his cattle in the hills, the son came upon a small lake where, to his astonishment, he saw "one of the most beautiful creatures that mortal eyes had ever beheld . . . a lady sitting on the unruffled surface of the water . . . arranging her tresses with a comb and using the glassy surface as a mirror." Suddenly she caught sight of the young man, staring at her steadily and holding out a piece of bread in the hope of luring her to shore. She approached but, refusing the bread because it was too hard, she dove under the water when he tried to grasp her. He returned home and came back the following day when, upon his mother's advice, he offered the lady some unbaked dough; but the result was no better.

Not till the third day, when he tried half-baked bread, did the lady accept it, and even encourage him to take her hand. Then, after a little persuasion, she agreed to become his bride, but on condition that they should live together only until she received from him "three blows without a cause." He acceded very willingly to this, whereupon she vanished again beneath the water. Immediately afterward, however, there emerged two beautiful ladies just like her, together with a hoary headed man of imposing stature who introduced himself as the bride's father and said that he would consent to the union if the young man could choose the right lady of the two. This was no easy task since they were so much alike but he finally recognized his beloved by the way her sandals were tied. Then her father promised her a dowry of as many sheep, cattle, goats, and horses as she could count "without heaving or drawing breath," and as she counted the animals came up out of the lake. After that the couple went to live on a nearby farm and dwelt there in prosperity and happiness, and three sons were born to them.

One day they were invited to a christening. The wife had no desire to go but the husband insisted, and when she was slow to bring the horses in from the field, he gave her a jocular slap on the shoulder with his glove, at which she reminded him of their agreement.

On another occasion when they were together at a wedding, she burst into tears in the midst of the cheerful company, and when her husband, tapping her on the shoulder, asked the reason for this, she replied: "Now trouble begins for this couple, and for you, too, because this is the second blow." After a time it happened that they attended a burial and, in contrast to the general mourning, she fell into fits of immoderate laughter. Naturally this was very trying to her husband, so he hit her and admonished her not to laugh. She said that she had laughed because people, when they die, are rid of their cares; and then she arose and left the house with these words: "The last blow has been struck; our marriage is broken and at an end. Farewell."

Then, calling together all her animals from the farm, she wended her way with the whole herd back to the lake and dove in.

The story does not say what happened to the disconsolate husband but relates that the sons often wandered about the vicinity of the lake and that their mother sometimes appeared to them there. Indeed she revealed to the oldest that he would benefit humanity by becoming a healer. She gave him a sack of medical prescriptions for this purpose and promised that she would come whenever he needed her advice. In fact she showed herself frequently and taught her sons the qualities of the healing herbs, so that they attained great celebrity by their medical knowledge and skill.

The last descendants of this family of physicians are said to have died in 1719 and 1739.

The story is, therefore, not solely concerned with an instinctual, erotic relationship; the water woman brings her husband prosperity and transmits to her sons a knowledge of healing herbs which is obviously due to her connection with nature.

Rhys cites countless similar legends connected with definite persons who trace their descent to water women and are proud of it. The taboos are not always the same; sometimes the man may not touch his wife with iron,[36] or he may not speak unfriendly words more than three times, and so on. But always the violation of the condition results from heedlessness, or a fateful accident; it is never intentional.

Irrational as these conditions may be in themselves, the effect that follows from infringing them is as consistent and invariable as a natural law. For half-human beings like these are part of nature and do not possess the freedom of choice allowed to man, which enables him sometimes to behave in a way that does not correspond to nature's laws, as, for example, when his behavior is determined by insights and feelings which raise it above the purely natural.

Much is to be learned in this story from the three incidents in which the water fairy receives the fatal blows.

The first occasion is a christening, which she has no wish

to take part in, and this means that the Christian rite is repugnant to her heathen nature. According to the ideas of that time, elfin beings shied away from everything Christian; the sermons of the Christian missionaries were said to have driven them off and caused them to withdraw into the earth (into what were called fairy hills).

In the second incident she bursts into tears on a joyful occasion, and in the third she disturbs the mood of mourning with unruly laughter; she behaves in an unadapted way and her utterances, although they seem reasonable to her, do not suit the circumstances. This is an indication that something undifferentiated is being expressed, because still unconscious or repressed elements of the personality remain primitive and undifferentiated, and when outwardly manifested (in this form), *telle quelle,* are unadapted. Similar manifestations can be inwardly observed or experienced by anyone at any time. The nixie who lives in the water, that is, in the unconscious, represents the feminine in a semi-human, almost unconscious state. In so far as she is married to a man, one may assume that she represents his unconscious, natural anima, together with his undifferentiated feeling, since her transgressions occur in this realm. At the same time it must be noted that she is unadapted not to matters of individual but of collective feeling. It is a fact that one's unconscious personality components (the anima, animus, and shadow), or one's inferior functions, are always those which the world finds offensive, and which are therefore repressed again and again. The nixie's disappearance into her element describes what happens when an unconscious content comes to the surface but is still so little coordinated with the ego consciousness as to sink back at the slightest provocation. That so little should be required to bring this about shows how fugacious and easily hurt these contents are.

In this context, too, belongs the revenge which elfin beings take when they are despised or insulted, for they are extremely touchy and likely to persevere in resentments unmodified by any human understanding. The same may be said of the anima, the animus and the undifferentiated functions; indeed, the exaggerated touchiness frequently to be met with in otherwise robust men is a sign of anima involvement. Likewise to be discerned in the anima are the incalculability, mischievousness and frequent malice of these elemental spirits, which constitute the reverse side of their bewitching charm. These beings are simply irrational, good and bad, helpful and harmful, healing and destructive, like nature herself of which they are a part.[37]

And the anima, as the unconscious, feminine aspect of man, is not alone in showing these qualities; the same can be seen in many women. For woman, in general, because of her biological task, has remained a more elemental being than man, and often manifests this kind of behavior more or less plainly. It is easy for a man to project the anima image to the more elemental women; they correspond so exactly to his own unconscious femininity.

Because of this, elemental creatures, preferably nixies, also appear often in the imagery of women's dreams and phantasies. They may represent either the undeveloped and still natural femininity of the woman concerned, or else her inferior function; often, however, they are incipient forms of the higher personality, of the Self.

In this legend we meet another characteristic feature, namely, the water maiden combing her hair — like the Lorelei — and mirroring herself in the lake. The combing of the hair can without difficulty be recognized as a means of sexual allurement still in use today. Looking in the mirror belongs with it, and the two actions together are often attributed to the anima figure in literature and the plastic arts.[38]

But the mirror as an attribute of the anima figure has still another meaning. One function of the anima is to be a looking glass for a man, to reflect his thoughts, desires, and emotions, as did the Valkyries. That is precisely why she is so important to him, whether as an inner figure or projected to an actual, outer woman; in this way he becomes aware of things about which he is still unconscious. Often, to be sure, this functioning of the anima does not lead to greater consciousness and self-knowledge, but merely to a self-mirroring which flatters the man's vanity, or even to a sentimental self-pity. Both naturally enhance the power of the anima and are therefore not without danger. Yet it is part of feminine nature to serve man as a mirror, and the astonishing adroitness that the woman often develops for this is what fits her especially to carry the man's anima projection.

The fair Melusine, also, belonged to the race of water fairies,[39] and, although the legend about her is well known, it contains several important points, so I will give it briefly.[40]

Raymond, adopted son of the Count of Poitiers, had killed the Count in a hunting accident and fled into the woods in unconsolable grief. There in a clearing he came upon three beautiful maidens sitting beside a spring, one of whom was Melusine. He poured out his sorrow to her and she gave him good counsel, whereupon he fell in love with her and asked her to marry him. She agreed upon one condition, that he would allow her to spend every Saturday in complete seclusion without ever intruding upon her. He accepted this and they lived happily together for many years. She bore him several sons, who all, however, had something abnormal and monstrous about them. She also had a splendid castle built and named it "Lusinia" after herself, although later it came to be known as Lusignan. Then one Saturday, disquieted by rumors that had reached him about his wife, Raymond spied upon her and, finding her in her bath chamber, saw to his horror that she had the tail of a fish or sea-serpent. At first this discovery seemed to make no difference, but a little later news came that one of Melusine's sons had attacked and burned a monastery which she had founded, and that another of the sons, who was a monk there, had perished. She tried to console her husband, but he pushed her aside saying: "Away, odious serpent, contaminator of my honorable race!" At these words she fainted. But when she recovered she took tearful leave of her husband and commended the children to his care; then, flying out of the window, she vanished "with a long wail of agony." Later she reappeared occasionally to look after the children, some of whom were still small, and for a long while the legend persisted that she would reappear over the ramparts of the castle whenever one of the Lords of Lusignan, who were supposed to be her descendants, was about to die.

Melusine's condition was that she be allowed once a week to return to her element and resume her nixie form. This is the secret which may not be spied upon. The non-human, the natural, in this case the fish tail, must not be seen. It is reasonable to assume that the weekly bath with its return to the natural state is equivalent to a renewal of life. Water is, indeed, the life element par excellence. It is indispensable for the preservation of life, and healing baths or springs which bring about the recovery and renewal of life have always been held numinous, and have often enjoyed religious veneration.[41] But the cults of trees, stones and springs, and the burning of fires and lights beside them were prohibited as heathen practises[42] by the council of Avignon in the year 442 A.D. In their stead images of the Virgin, decorated with flowers and candles, are raised near springs in many places as Christian expressions of the ancient feeling that still survives even today. One cognomen of Mary is *"pégé,"* which means spring. The numinous quality of water is also expressed by the very old concept of a "water of life" possessing supernatural power, or the *"aqua permanens"* of the alchemists. Nymphs or fairies, dwelling in or near springs, have a special affinity with the water, which is believed to be the life element, and, since the source of life is an unsolved mystery, so the nymph, too, has about her something mysterious which must remain hidden. In a sense these beings are the guardians of the springs and certain healing springs have a patron saint to this day: Baden, for example, has St. Verena, who replaced a pagan nymph and is also connected with Venus.

The anima, whose name expresses her animating character, fulfils a similar function. So she often appears in dreams or phantasies as this kind of fairy being. For instance, a young man, who was very rational in his attitude and therefore exposed to the danger of dessication, dreamed as follows:

"I am going through a dense wood; then, there comes toward me a woman enveloped in a dark veil, who takes me by the hand and says that she will lead me to the wellspring of life."

Recounting an early experience, the English writer William Sharp[43] (1855-1905) tells of a beautiful white woman of the woods who appeared to him beside a small lake encircled with plane trees. As a child he called her "Star-Eyes," later "Lady of the Sea," and he says that he knew her "to be no other than the woman who is in the heart of all women." Plainly, she is the primal image of womanhood, an unmistakable anima figure.[44]

The anima represents the connection with the spring or source of life in the unconscious. When no such connection exists, or when it is broken, a state of stagnation or torpor results, often so disturbing that it causes the person involved to seek out a psychiatrist. Gottfried Keller describes this condition most impressively in his poem, "Winter Night."[45]

"Not a wing beat in the winter sky,
    Still and dazzling white the fallen snow.
    Not a cloudlet veiled the stars on high;
    No wave stirred the frozen lake below.

"From the deep rose up a water-tree
    Till its top froze in the icy screen;
    On a branch a nixie climbed toward me,
    Gazing upward through the frigid green.

"Standing there upon the glassy sheet
    Parting me from depths so black and dim,
    I could see, now close beneath my feet
    Her white beauty gleaming, limb by limb.

"She, in muffled misery, probed to find
    In that rigid roof some fissured space —
    She is always, always, in my mind;
    Never will I forget her shadowy face."

The nixie, imprisoned in ice, corresponds to the enchanted princess in the glass mountain, who was mentioned above; both glass and ice form a cold, hard, and rigid armor, imprisoning what is living so that it needs to be set free.

Still another important feature of the Melusine legend should be mentioned. When her son sets fire to the monastery that Melusine has founded, this obviously expresses the antagonism already referred to between the elfin race and Christianity. On the other hand, according to many accounts, it appears that these beings also desired redemption.

Paracelsus, who wrote a whole treatise on such elemental spirits as nymphs, sylphs, pigmies, and salamanders, says that although they do indeed resemble human beings, they are not descended from Adam, and have no souls. The water people are the most like men and try the hardest to enter into connections with humans. They "have not only been truly seen

by man, but have married him and have borne him children."[46]
And further: "It is said of the nymphs, that they come to us
from the water, and sit on the banks of the brooks where they
have their abode, where they are seen, taken also, caught and
married, as we said before."[47] Through union with a man they
receive a soul and the children, too, of such unions possess
souls. "From this it follows that they woo man, and that they
seek him assiduously and in secret,"[47] in the same way that a
"heathen begs for baptism and woos it in order to acquire his
soul and to become alive in Christ."

These disquisitions by Paracelsus provided the material for
F. de la Motte Fouqué's *Undine*,[48] written at the beginning
of the nineteenth century, that is, in the Romantic period,
when the idea of a soul informing nature was revived, and also
when the idea of the unconscious was first talked about.[49] In
this story the central motif is the soullessness of the nixie.

Undine is the daughter of a sea king who reigns in the Mediter-
ranean. At his wish, so that she may acquire a soul, she is secretly
brought to a fisher couple, who, believing that their own child
has drowned, take the foundling instead. Undine grows up a
charming girl, yet often alienates her foster parents by her strangely
childish nature, her constant inclination to mischievous tricks.

During a storm an errant knight seeks shelter in the fisherman's
hut, and Undine, though usually wayward and shy, is confidingly
friendly toward him. Her charm and childlike ways enchant him
and, since the storm has conveniently deflected a reverend father
to the hut, the pair are wedded by him. But now Undine admits
to her husband that she has no soul, and he begins to feel uneasy.
Despite all his love, he is plagued by the thought of being married
to an elfin being. She begs him not to cast her off, since her kind
cannot win souls except through a bond of human love. She asks
one thing of him only, that he will never — particularly if they
are near the water — say a harsh word to her, since, if he does, the
water people who are her guardians will come and fetch her away.

The knight takes her home to his castle, and then fate appears in the figure of Berthalda, a damsel who had hoped to become his wife. Undine receives her in friendly fashion, but the knight grows increasingly uneasy. Finally, while they are boating on the Danube, this uneasiness finds expression in his accusing Undine of witchcraft and jugglery when, in place of Berthalda's necklace that had fallen into the water, she lifts out a string of corals.[50] Deeply hurt, Undine swings herself from the boat and disappears weeping beneath the flowing water, but not before warning her husband that if he fails to remain true to her the water spirits will take revenge.

Nevertheless his marriage to Berthalda is soon planned. On the wedding day Berthalda asks to have her beauty lotion brought from the castle well, which previously had been sealed on Undine's order, to prevent the water spirits from coming in. When the stone is removed, Undine's figure emerges veiled in white. Weeping, she moves toward the castle and knocks softly at her husband's window. In a mirror he sees her entering and approaching him. As she nears his couch, she says: "They have opened the well, so I am come, and now you must die." Unveiling herself, she takes him in her arms and he dies as she kisses him.[51]

What brings about the catastrophe here is the conflict between the anima, that is the nature creature, and the human woman. In the Siegfried legend this plays an important part, as the strife between the Valkyrie Brünnehilde and Chriemhilde, and it frequently leads to great difficulties in actual life. Fundamentally, such conflict expresses that opposition between two worlds, the outer and the inner, the conscious and the unconscious, which it seems to be the special task of our time to bridge.

Another type of anima experience is presented in *"Le Lai de Lanval,"*[52] which is part of the Breton cycle of legends.

Lanval was a knight belonging to King Arthur's company, but he felt disregarded because he had not sufficient wealth to make a fine display. One day, however, he met a beautiful damsel by a spring; she led him to her yet more beautiful mistress, who entertained him wondrously and bestowed upon him the favor of her love. Her only condition was that he should never betray any part of it. She also promised to fulfil his every wish and to appear whenever he desired her. Thanks to this his other longings were gratified, and he was able to fit himself out so handsomely as to gain more and more consideration at court. He even attracted the attention of the queen, who offered him her love. When he refused this, she was so hurt that she finally forced him to admit that he had a mistress more beautiful than herself. Angrily, she demanded that the king should call Lanval before a court of judgment to defend himself against the charge of having insulted the queen. To do so he would have to prove that his mistress was really as beautiful as he said. But the difficulty was that now he could no longer summon the lady, because he had betrayed the secret of her love. All hope seemed lost when, accompanied by four fair damsels and riding upon a splendidly caparisoned white palfrey, his beloved appeared, like beauty in person, garbed in white and wearing a purple mantle. Lanval was now justified; all were compelled to admit that he had not claimed too much. The song ends with the fairy taking her love away on the horse to her kingdom.[53]

Being carried away to fairyland is, psychologically, a very important motif. In the Celtic tradition this realm does not have the terrible and fearful character that it possesses elsewhere. It is not a kingdom of the dead but is called "Land of the Living" or "Land under the Waves," and is thought to be composed of "green islands," which are inhabited by fair feminine beings and so sometimes called "islands of women."[54] Eternally young and beautiful, these creatures enjoy a life without sorrow, full of music and dancing and the joys of love. The fairies live here, including famed Morgan la Fée (Fata Morgana) whose name implies that she is "seaborn," and thither they lead their human lovers. Psychologically, this Elysium, comparable to the Gardens of the Hesperides, can be interpreted as a dream land, which is alluring and pleasant, to be sure, but not without peril. That the anima rules this realm and leads the way to it is well known. The danger of getting lost there, that is, in the unconscious, seems to have been felt even in early times, for countless stories describe the knight, caught in the bonds of love, who forgets his knightly duties[55] and in a self-sufficient twosome with his lady becomes estranged from the world and from reality.

An extreme example of this kind is the case of the enchanter Merlin, whose beloved, the fairy Vivian, used the magic arts which she had learned by eavesdropping upon him, to tie him in invisible bonds and imprison him in a hawthorn bush from which he was never able to escape.

This story is particularly instructive because the figure of Merlin so very fittingly embodied the consciousness and the thinking faculty which were lacking in the masculine world around him. He was a Luciferian, Mephisto-like being, and as such represented the intellect in *statu nascendi,* that is, in still primitive form. To this he owed his magic power; but because his feminine side had been neglected, it drew him back in the form of eros, and bound in the toils of nature this man who had identified himself with the logos principle.

To a somewhat later period belongs the Tannhäuser legend which Richard Wagner revived; it apparently dates from the fifteenth century and was widely known in the sixteenth throughout Switzerland, Germany, and the Netherlands.[56]

> "Now is forsooth my lay begun
> Of Danhauser I'll sing thee,
> And of the wonders he hath done
> With Venus, the noble Minnie.[57]

> "Danhauser was a sturdy knight
> In quest of wonders he
> Did wish to enter Venus' mount,
> Where pretty women be."

That is the way most versions of the song begin, but there
is a Swiss form from St. Gallen, accounted one of the oldest,
which says:

> "Danuser was ein wundrige Knab
> Grauss Wunder got er go schaue
> Er got wol uf der Frau Vrenesberg[58]
> Zu dene dri schöne Jungfraue.

> "Die sind die ganze Wuche gar schö
> Mit Gold und mit Side behange,
> Händ Halsschmeid a und Maiekrö
> *Am Suntig sind s' Otre und Schlange!*"[59]

Whereby the residents of the Venusberg are marked as rela-
tives of Melusine.

Though I believe I may assume that the legend is familiar,
let us recall the circumstances.

After Tannhäuer had lingered for a long while in the Venusberg, his conscience smote him and he went to Rome to ask for
absolution from the Pope. But this was denied him and he was
told that his sin would no more be forgiven than the dead branch
before him would become green again. So he returned to the
Venusberg and remained there, even when the Pope sent him a
messenger with tidings that a miracle had occurred, that the
branch had grown green once more. The end of the song, in many
versions, goes as follows:

> "Thus he within the mount again
> Doth choose her love to be,
> And to the Pope, the fourth Urban,
> Is lost eternally."[60]

As the name shows, Venusberg is a place of love's pleasures
and delights where Venus hold sway.[61] It corresponds in every
way to the "islands of women" or the fairy hills, spoken of

earlier, and all the legends about it resemble each other closely in that they tell of a man being lured to such a place and held there by a woman's enchantment, and of his never, or only with the greatest difficulty, being able to find his way out again.

An example of this in antiquity was Calypso, who held Odysseus on her island and released him only at the behest of the gods. The enchantress Circe belongs in this category, too; but her character was more witch-like, since she changed her victims, Odysseus' comrades, into swine.

The antagonism between Christianity and paganism, already intimated in the story of Melusine, comes clearly to light in the Tannhäuser legend. However, the paganism which emerged at the time of the Renaissance was not that of the northern peoples, but that of antiquity. An example suited to our theme is the famous *Hipnerotomachia Poliphili* of Francesco Colonna.[62] Here a monk describes how, in a dream, his beloved, the nymph Polia, after letting him see and experience a series of psychologically significant scenes and images from classical antiquity, finally leads him to Cytherea, where Venus gives the pair of them her blessing.

Another work important to mention here is *Le Paradis de la Reyne Sibylle* by Antoine de la Sale.[63] It was preserved in two fifteenth century manuscripts and printed in 1521. This "paradise," according to one Italian tradition, lies on the Monte della Sibilla in the Appennines. The author, who had visited the place, gives an account of it and of the traditions connected with it. A cave in the mountain is supposed to be the entrance to Queen Sibylle's palace and her realm within corresponds exactly to the Venusberg. The legend resembles that of Tannhauser, except that here the repentant knight is promised immediate forgiveness for his sins. However, his squire leads him to believe that the pope is deceiving him and really intends to imprison them, so they both return to the sibyl's paradise.

That in this story the queen and her maidens should retire, every Friday at midnight, to their chambers for twenty-four hours and assume snake forms is a feature already familiar to us from the Melusine legend. I regret that the space at my disposal does not permit me to discuss the book further. However, it is interesting in the light of what has already been said to note that in this tradition the Venusberg and the sibyl's mountain are identical. According to Desonay the sibyl referred to is the Cumaean one, who told Aeneas the way to the underworld, explaining where the golden branch could be found that would open its entrance.[64] This was supposed to be in a cave near Lake Avernus, and a grotto said to be the sibyl's is still shown in the vicinity. Obviously the tradition has been combined with that of the cave on the Monte della Sibilla, which also lies near a lake and was believed to lead to Queen Sibylle's paradise.[65]

But there is still more: Desonay[66] conjectures that possibly this grotto may once have been dedicated to Cybele, the mother of the gods, whose cult in 204 B.C. was introduced into Rome as the result of a saying in the Sibylline Books, and subsequently spread as far as northern Italy and Gaul.[67] As life bestower and goddess of fertility, Cybele ruled the waters; as Mountain Mother and Mistress of Animals, she loved and ruled all that was wild in nature. She bestowed the gift of prophecy, but caused madness also, and her orgiastic cult was related to that of Dionysus.[68] She is familiar to us as the mother of Attis, but to go further into that myth now would lead us too far. I want only to recall that part of the cult of this goddess was that the priests should emasculate themselves. As we have seen, those held prisoner in the fairy realm[69] experienced the equivalent of emasculation, too, losing their virility and

becoming womanlike and soft. The great difference, however, is that whereas they *succumbed* to temptation and were
subdued by feminine magic, the priests of Cybele *offered* a
sacrifice to the goddess.

Unquestionably the character of the goddess Cybele can be
compared to that of the "Reyne Sibylle," even if Desonay's
hypothesis is not substantiated by archaeological findings.

This sibyl's paradise contains almost all the features previously noted in the various stories of swan maidens, nixies and
fairies. That a complex of ideas, such as this, should have
existed all over the world since primeval times, always recurring in the same combination or else simply remaining un-
changed, clearly indicates that the material with which we
are dealing is basically archetypal.

The *Great Mother*, the *Prophetess* and the *Love Goddess*
are all aspects of primal femininity and also, therefore, aspects
of the anima archetype.

According to Kerényi's conclusions,[70] Cybele and Aphrodite
are in the last analysis one and the same figure, and both may
be equated to the great nature goddess. Hers, too, is the divine
figure reflected in the elemental creatures described above and
in the legends associated with them, the same figure whose
traits the anima likewise shares.

But swan maidens and nixies are not the only forms in
which elemental feminine nature shows itself. Melusine is
scolded by her husband for being a "serpent," and this figure,
too, can embody the primal feminine. It represents a more
primitive and chthonic femininity than the fish does, for example, and certainly more than the bird, while at the same
time cleverness, even wisdom, is ascribed to it. Moreover, the
serpent is also dangerous. Its bite is poisonous and its embrace
suffocating,[71] yet everyone knows that despite this dangerousness the effect that it exerts is fascinating.

Appearing in countless myths and fairy tales, the serpent's role is not always expressly feminine. In modern dreams and phantasies, of men as well as of women, it often stands for pre-human and undifferentiated libido rather than for a psychic component that is conscious or capable of becoming conscious.[72]

Yet there are certainly instances where the serpent has an expressly anima character. In discussing the psychological aspects of the Kore figure,[73] Jung tells of a young man's dream about a female snake which behaved "tenderly and insinuatingly" and spoke to him in a human voice. Another man, who sometimes sees a ringed snake in his garden, says that he feels it looks at him with remarkably human eyes, as if it wanted to make a relation with him.

The spirit of nature also appears as a snake or as a "golden green triple snakeling," in the story of "The Golden Pot" by E. T. A. Hoffmann.[74] Here the little snake, which looks at the hero of the tale with "inexpressible yearning," turns into Serpentina, a real anima figure who possesses the golden pot. The pot is a vessel in which "the wonderful land of Atlantis" is mirrored and this land, being sunk in the sea, represents the unconscious. In letting the hero behold such images, Serpentina fulfils a typical anima function, and besides this she helps him to decipher some enigmatic writing found on an emerald green leaf, which is not hard to recognize as a leaf from nature's book.

Whenever the anima appears as a beast of prey, as often happens in dreams and phantasies, it is her dangerousness that is being stressed. A man, for example, may dream that a lioness which has left her cage approaches and circles ingratiatingly around him. Then she turns into a woman, becomes threatening and wants to devour him. Tigers, panthers, leopards, and beasts of prey, generally, appear in this kind of dream. In

China the female fox plays a big role; she likes to present herself as a beautiful maiden, but her tail can be recognized. Often there is something ghostly about her and she is taken to be the embodiment of a departed spirit. Women have similar dreams, but in their case the animal, in so far as it is female, represents the shadow or the primitive femininity of the dreamer.

In recent literature the figure of Antinea in Benoit's novel, *L'Atlantide*,[75] most impressively reveals both the serpent and the beast-of-prey aspects of the elemental anima. Fascinating all the men who come her way with the beauty of Venus, the wisdom of the serpent, and the cruelty of the carnivore, she works irresistible magic upon them and without exception they perish. Then their mummified corpses are used to ornament a mausoleum erected especially for the purpose. Antinea claims to have risen from the Lost Atlantis and to be descended from Neptune; hence, like Morgan la Fée and Aphrodite, she is sea-born. She is a purely destructive anima figure; those whom she enchants lose all of their masculine strength and virtue and finally die.

As may be seen from these examples, succumbing to the power of the anima always has the same fatal effect and is in a way comparable to the emasculation of the priests of Cybele.

That Antinea should explain her nefarious behavior as revenge upon man, who for centuries has exploited woman and misused her, is psychologically significant. In so far as she embodies negative archetypal femininity, this would be the feminine principle revenging itself for the devaluation to which it has been subjected.

When, as happens in so many legends, an elemental creature seeks to unite with a human being and be loved by him in order to acquire a soul, it can only mean that some unconscious and undeveloped component of the personality is seeking to become joined to consciousness and so to be informed with soul. This striving is expressed in the same way in dreams, and C. G. Jung gives an example of the kind:[76]

A young man dreams that a white bird flies into the window of his room. It turns into a little girl about seven years old who, after perching herself on the table beside him, changes back into a bird again, but still speaks with a human voice.

This shows that a feminine creature wants admission to the dreamer's house; but it is still a child, that is, undeveloped; this is also expressed by the fact that it becomes a bird again. It is a first clear appearance of the anima figure, emerging to the threshold of consciousness, but only half-human as yet.

For the unconscious has not only a tendency to persist in its primal state and to engulf and extinguish what has already been made conscious;[77] it also shows plain signs of activity in the opposite direction. There are unconscious contents that struggle to become conscious and, like elves, revenge themselves if this is not taken into account. The urge toward increased consciousness seemingly proceeds from the archetypes, as though, so to speak, there were an instinct tending toward this goal. But where such an impulse comes from, or what the nature of the dynamis is which sets it going, we do not know. It belongs among the undiscovered secrets of the psyche and of life.

The urge toward increase of consciousness in the material discussed above is expressed in the desire of a creature, still bound to nature and only half human, to approach a human being and be accepted by him, that is, by consciousness. In this connection, perhaps another motif which has not yet been mentioned deserves consideration; namely, the fact that these elemental beings quite often possess a (more or less hidden) father. The Valkyries are Odin's maidens and Odin is a god of wind and spirit. In the tale of the huntsman and the swan maiden, who has to be released from the glass mountain, her father is with her and is released at the same time. The Welsh nixie's father gives her in marriage to the man, and Undine, too, is sent by the sea-king, her father, to live among men in order to gain a soul.

In modern dreams and active imagination, the anima also appears frequently in the company of a father figure. This can be taken as an intimation that behind the feminine nature-element there lies a masculine-spiritual factor, to which may be ascribed the knowledge of hidden things possessed by these elemental feminine creatures. Jung calls this factor "the Old Wise Man," or the "archetype of meaning," while he designates the anima as the "archetype of life."[78]

The meaningful factor in the unconscious is what makes it possible for consciousness to develop. In a certain sense this factor is comparable to the idea of the *lumen naturae*, which Paracelsus describes as an invisible light that "reaches man, as in a dream." He says that "since the light of Nature can not speak, it buildeth shapes in sleep from the power of the Word (of God)."[79]

Reviewing all that has been said about these elemental creatures, we see that in general they possess the same qualities and behave in similar ways. Moreover, these qualities and the effects they produce can well be likened to those of the anima. *Both the nature creature and the anima represent the eros principle, the former transmitting hidden knowledge, just as the latter transmits information about the contents of the unconscious.* Both exert a fascinating effect and often possess a power overwhelming enough to produce ruinous results, especially when certain conditions affecting the relationship between the human being and the elemental one, or between the conscious ego and the anima, are left unfulfilled. This failure is the reason why many legends end unsatisfactorily, that is, with the relationship broken off or made impossible. From this it may be seen that such a tie is a delicate matter, as is also the relation to the anima. Indeed, we know from experience that the anima makes certain demands upon a man. She is a psychic factor that insists on being considered, not neglected as is the general tendency, since a man naturally likes to identify himself with his masculinity.

However, it is not a question of either surrendering his masculinity completely to the service of the Lady Anima or losing her entirely, but only of granting a certain space to the feminine, which is also a part of his being. This he does by recognizing and realizing the eros, the principle of relationship, which means that he not only becomes aware of his feeling, but also makes use of it, because to create, and especially to preserve, a relationship, a value judgment (which is what feeling is) cannot be dispensed with. A man by nature tends to relate to objects, to his work, or to some other field of interest; but what matters to a woman is the personal relation, and this is true also of the anima. Her tendency is to entangle a man in such relationships, but she can also serve him well in giving them shape — that is, she can do so after the feminine element has been incorporated into consciousness. As long as this element works autonomously, it disturbs relations or makes them impossible.

The researches and discoveries of depth psychology have shown that for modern people (or at least for many of them) a coming to terms with the unconscious is essential. To a man the relation with the anima is of special importance; to a woman, that with the animus. These factors, by building a sort of bridge, establish the connection with the unconscious in general. The anima as a rule is projected first upon a real woman; this may lead the man to enter upon a relation with her that he might otherwise find impossible; on the other hand, it may also result in his becoming much too dependent upon her, with the fatal results described above.

As long as such a projection exists it is naturally difficult for the man to find a relation to the inner anima, to his own femininity. Yet figures of women that cannot be identified with actual persons often occur in dreams. They appear usually as the "stranger," the "unknown" or the "veiled woman," or, as in the legends, they take the form of not quite human creatures. Dreams of this kind are likely to make a strong impression and be colored with feeling; it is easy to believe that they concern an inner psychic magnitude with which a relationship must be established.

In literature there is a contrast between the great number of figures like this, with all their attendant circumstances and effects, and the rarity of cases in which relationships between men and such elemental creatures are brought to a satisfactory conclusion. This may result from lack of sufficient consciousness in the human being. It is essential in establishing a relation to the unconscious that the ego be strong and well-defined enough to resist the danger, always present when one deals with the unconscious, of being overwhelmed and extinguished by it.[80] A clearly defined ego is also needed to maintain the continuity of a relation of this kind, for although the unconscious figures would like to be accepted by men, that is, admitted into consciousness, they are by nature fugacious and easily disappear again. (As Urvasî says: "I have passed away like the first of the dawns . . . I am like the wind difficult to catch.")

Yet the solution of this problem appears to be a task of special urgency today, as psychotherapists and psychologists can testify, and in the method known as active imagination C. G. Jung has pointed out an approach to it.[81] The confrontation and coming to terms of the ego personality with these figures of the unconscious serve on the one hand to differentiate them from the ego, on the other, to relate them to it, and both sides are affected.

A good and very charming example of this is to be found in "Libussa," an originally Czech fairy tale, newly edited by Musaeus.[82] Briefly, the story is as follows:

A tree nymph, seeing her oak endangered, obtains protection from a young and noble squire named Krokus. For his service she proposes to reward him with the fulfilment of a wish: for fame and honor, perhaps, or riches, or happiness in love. But he chooses none of these, desiring instead "to rest in the shade of the oak from the weary marching of war," and there from the mouth of the nymph to learn "lessons of wisdom for unriddling the secrets of the future." This wish is granted and every evening at twilight she comes to him and they wander together along the reedy shores of a pond. "She instructed her attentive pupil," we are told, "in Nature's secrets, taught him the origin and essence of things, their natural and magical qualities, and so transformed the crude warrior into a thinker and a man of world-embracing wisdom. *In the degree that the young man's sensitivity and feeling became refined by his association with this fair elf, her fragile, shadowy figure seemed to take on additional solidity and substance.* Her breast gained warmth and life, her brown eyes sparkled fire and, along with this womanly aspect, she seemed also to acquire the feelings of blossoming maidenhood."

Here is an unusually apt description of the effects and counter-effects resulting from a relationship with the anima figure. She becomes more real and more alive; while the man's feeling undergoes a differentiation, and he is taught, too, to become "a thinker and a man of world-embracing wisdom," thereby achieving fame. The story comes to a natural conclusion;[83] after they have lived together for a long time, the nymph one day says farewell to her husband, foreseeing that the end of her oak tree can no longer be averted. Then the tree is struck by lightning and she, whose life has remained bound to it despite her human quality, disappears forever.

A remarkable and, I believe, unique relation to the anima was found by William Sharp,[84] the English author I have already mentioned. At the wish of his merchant father he first studied law but proved unsuited to it. Then he spent three years, equally unsatisfactorily, in a London banking house. Resigning this position, he turned to art and literary criticism and also published some poems. These occupations brought him into touch with London literary and artistic circles and he became especially friendly with Dante Gabriel Rossetti. In the biography from which this material is taken (written by his wife who was also his cousin) we are told that university teaching posts were repeatedly offered to him which he could not accept because of his health. Besides this critical and intellectual side, he had also a lively life of dreams and phantasies which he called the "green life," because it was so closely connected with nature, for which he cherished a great love. This side of his character came into its own during his annual trips to the sea, and above all in Scotland. In his boyhood a Scottish nurse had familiarized him with Gaelic legends, and Scotland for him seemed a home of the soul. During one stay there he started writing a Celtic romance entitled *Pharais,* he became aware as he wrote of the predominance of the feminine element in it, and of how much the book owed its inception to the subjective, feminine side of his nature. In consequence he decided to publish it under the name Fiona Macleod, which came "ready made" to his mind; subsequently he wrote a number of other books under this pseudonym, vividly rendering the special character of Scotland and its inhabitants. Due to the awakening of a new interest in Celtic things among a group of writers at this period, these were very well received. According to William Butler Yeats, among the new voices none was more distinctive than the mysterious and remarkable voice revealing itself in the stories of Fiona Macleod, which seemed itself to become the voices of these simple people and elemental things — not by observation of them only, but by identity of nature. The art of these stories, Yeats said, was of the kind that rested upon revelation; it dealt with invisible, ungraspable things. Asked why he wrote under a woman's name, Sharp replied, "I can write out of my heart in a way I could not do as William Sharp . . . This rapt sense of oneness with nature, this *cosmic ecstasy* and elation, this wayfaring along the extreme verges of the common world, all this is so wrought up with the romance of life that I could not bring myself to expression by my outer self . . ."[85] He made a close secret of his identity with Fiona Macleod and for a long while not even his friends were made acquainted with "her"; William Sharp had his own correspondence, and Fiona Macleod kept up a separate one with her readers. To his wife he wrote: "More and more absolutely, in one sense, are W. S. and F. M. becoming two persons — often married in mind and one nature, but often absolutely distinct;"[86] and he signed this letter "Wilfion" (a contraction of William and Fiona). Sometimes, too, on his birthday he exchanged letters with Fiona, in which he expressed gratitude to her and she gave him advice.

Here we have a case where the inner anima attained a rare degree of reality. Perhaps this was due to a special disposition on the part of William Sharp; in principle, however, it corresponds to what we mean when we speak of relating to or integrating the anima — which, in a certain degree, is surely possible to all men.

For the integration of the anima, the feminine element, into a man's conscious personality is part of the individuation process. In this connection, however, a point of special importance must be taken into consideration, for the feminine element which must become an integrated component of the personality is only a portion of the anima, namely, its *personal* aspect. The anima also represents the archetype of womanhood, which is *suprapersonal* in nature and therefore cannot be integrated.

Behind the elemental beings of our study stand, as we have seen, the divine figures of Cybele and Aphrodite — in the last analysis, the Goddess Nature. This archetypal background explains the irresistible force which can emanate from such an anima figure; for if in it Nature herself is encountered, then it is understandable that a man may be overcome and fall into its power. This happens particularly when no differentiation is made between the archetypal and the personal aspects of the anima. Indeed, confusing the two aspects is what gives the anima superior power, and that is why it is most important to discriminate between what belongs to the personal and what to the suprapersonal. This separation is sometimes represented in dreams and phantasies by the death of the suprapersonal anima figure. I know of one phantasy in which she rises to heaven, and the ordinary woman remains behind; in *The Dream of Poliphilo,* which has already been mentioned, the dream closes with the nymph Polia dissolving "into thin air, like a heavenly image."[87]

C. G. Jung tells of a man's dream in which a female figure of more than life size and with a veiled face stands in a church — in the place of the altar. Indeed, like the Platonic ideas, the archetype of the anima is of superhuman nature and dwells in a celestial place. Though distinct from the personal, feminine components of the soul, she is nevertheless the primal image standing behind them and shaping them to her likeness.

As Great Mother and Goddess of Love, as "Mistress," or by whatever other name she may be called, the anima in her archetypal aspect is to be met with reverence. On the other hand, a man must come to terms with his personal anima, the femininity that belongs to him, that accompanies and supplements him but may not be allowed to rule him.

In attempting, as I have in this study, to present the anima as an elemental being, I have left out the higher forms of its manifestation as, for example, Sophia. This is because it seemed important to me to emphasize the natural aspect which so markedly belongs to the essence of feminine being.

When the anima is recognized and integrated a change of attitude occurs toward the feminine generally. This new evaluation of the feminine principle brings with it a due reverence for nature, too; whereas the intellectual viewpoint dominant in an era of science and technology leads to utilizing and even exploiting nature, rather than honoring her. Fortunately, signs can be observed today pointing in the latter direction. Most important and significant of these is probably the new dogma of the *Assumptio Mariae* and her proclamation as mistress of creation. In our time, when such threatening forces of cleavage are at work, splitting peoples, individuals, and atoms, it is doubly necessary that those which unite and hold together should become effective; for life is founded on the harmonious interplay of masculine and feminine forces, within the individual human being as well as without. Bringing these opposites into union is one of the most important tasks of present-day psychotherapy.

NOTES

1. *Lieder des Rig-Veda.* Translated into German by H. Hillebrandt. Göttingen: Vandenhoock & Ruprecht, 1913. X. 95, p. 142.
2. *Satapatha-Brahmana* in *Sacred Books of the East,* XLIV. Ed. F. Max Mueller. Oxford: Oxford University Press, 1900. p. 69 ff.

3. The Apsaras (those who move in water) are celestial water nymphs of great beauty, devoted to song and dance. Their masculine partners are the likewise music-loving Gandharvas. See Hastings. *Encyclopedia of Religion and Ethics,* under "Brahmanism."

4. Apuleius. *The Metamorphoses or The Golden Ass.* See Erich Neumann's *Amor and Psyche: The Psychic Development of the Feminine.* Bollingen Series LIV. New York: Pantheon Press, 1956.

5. Cf. Adalbert Kuhn. *Die Herabkunft des Feuers und des Göttertranks.* Berlin: Dummlers Verlag Buchhandlung, 1859. Here this son is conceived of as fire.

6. Johann W. Goethe. *Faust.* Translated by George M. Priest. New York: Alfred A. Knopf, 1950.

7. Taken from *A Celtic Miscellany.* Translated by K. H. Jackson. London: Routledge & Kegan Paul, 1951. Also, H. Arbois de Jubainville. *The Irish Mythological Cycle and Celtic Mythology.* Translated from the French by R. I. Best. Dublin: Hodges, Figgis & Co. Ltd., 1903.

8. Wilhelm K. Grimm. *Deutsche Mythologie.* Vol. I, Chaps. XVI, IV, 1835. This work has been republished, Vienna & Leipzig: Bernina Verlag, 1939. All the following references, however, are to the 1835 edition. (Ed. note)

9. One of Odin's names is *Wunsch* (Wish). W. *Grimm, ibid.,* Vol. I, Chap. XVI.

10. W. Grimm, *ibid.*

11. Cf. *Wayland Smith.* Translated from the French of Dopping and Michel by S. W. Singer. London: William Pickering, 1947. This English version was chosen because it most closely resembles the German used by Mrs. Jung, (*Edda.* Vol. I, Translated into German by Felix Genzmer. Jena: Diederichs Verlag, 1912). A few changes, however, have been required to make it correspond entirely. (Ed. note)

12. This means that, as Valkyries, they spun the threads of victory and fame.

13. Cf. also M.-L. von Franz. *Archetypal Patterns in Fairy Tales.* Zürich: Privately printed, 1951. Chap. V.

14. According to Grimm (*ibid.* Chap XII) the swan was considered a prophetic bird, and that the word *schwanen* is equivalent to *ahnen* (to have a presentiment) seems to have a connection with this. According to J. A. MacCulloch (*The Religion of the Ancient Celts.* Edinburgh: T. & T. Clark, 1911) the Badb, or "battle crow," an old war goddess of Irish mythology, is related to the Valkyries, but has the more sinister character of a foreteller of evil.

15. On the anima as a spinner, see C. G. Jung. *Aion.* Zürich: Rascher Verlag, 1951. An English translation of this section of *Aion* appeared

as "Shadow, Anima, and Animus" in *Spring 1950,* published by the Analytical Psychology Club of N.Y. Inc. p. 3.

16. *Udr, Verdandi* and *Skuld* are the past, present, and future of the verb, to be. See *Prose Edda.* Scandinavian Classics. Vol. V. New York: Oxford University Press, 1929. Notes 12, 13, 14, p. 28.

17. *Fatum* means statement, prophecy (See A. Walde. *Lateinisches Etymologisches Wörterbuch,* 1910).

18. *The Lay of the Nibelungs.* Metrically translated from the Old German text by Alice Horton. London: George Bell & Son, 1901. The following passage occurs in Adventure XXV, Verse 1536.

19. *"Sie swebten sam die Vogele vor im uf der vluot.*
    Des duhten in ir Sinne stare unde guot.
    Zwas si im sagen wolden, er geloubte in dester bas."

20. Tacitus. *Germania* 8. Quoted from W. Grimm *(ibid.,* Vol. I, Chap. V, p. 78).

21. *"ut matres familias eorum sortibus et vaticinationibus declararent utrum proelium committi ex usu esset nec ne."* Grimm, *ibid.,* Vol. I, Chap. V, p. 78.

22. Grimm, *ibid.,* Vol. I, p. 361.

23. *"quandam mulierem fatatam, sive quandam fatam, que alio nomine nimpha, vel dea, vel adriades (dryas) appelatur."*

24. "The Bologna Enigma" was published in English in *Ambix,* Vol. II; Journal of the Society for the Study of Alchemy and Early Chemistry. London: Dec. 1946.

25. Cf. C. G. Jung. "The Psychological Aspects of the Mother Archetype" in *Spring 1943* (published by the Analytical Psychology Club of N.Y. Inc.) and translated from the German in the *Eranos-Jahrbuch* VI. Zürich: Rhein Verlag, 1939.

26. *The Works of Plato.* Translated by B. Jowett. New York: Dial Press, No date. p. 401.

27. See in this connection, *"Der Jager und die Schwanjungfrau"* (The Huntsman and the Swan Maiden) in *Deutsche Märchen seit Grimm,* hrsg. von Paul Zaunert. Jena: Diederichs, 1919. See also *"Die weisse und die schwarze Braut"* (The White and the Black Bride) and *"Die Rabe"* (The Raven) from Grimm's *Kinder- und Hausmärchen,* Vols. I & II, and *"Die Entenjungfrau,"* (The Young Duck Woman) a Russian tale; all to be found in *Märchen der Weltliteratur.* Jena: Diederichs, 1915. Likewise "The Adventures of Hassan of Bassora," which is the tale of the 577th night in *The Book of the Thousand Nights and One Night.*

28. According to Germanic and Northern sources the glass mountain was thought of as a place in the Beyond, the dwelling of the dead or the blessed; according to other ideas, swan maidens, fairies, witches, dwarfs, and similar beings lived there. In many fairy tales people are led there by a spirit or demon and have to be redeemed. (Cf. *Handwörterbuch des deutschen Aberglaubens,* published by H.

Baechtold-Staubli, under *"Glasberg")* This place in the Beyond may
well be equated with the unconscious.

29. *"Der geraubte Schleier."* See J. K. Musaeus. *Volksmärchen der Deutschen,* Vol. II, in *Märchen der Weltliteratur. l. c.*

30. "Field of Swans." Here the editor injects the amusing remark that this locale got its name from a certain Schwanhildis and her father Cygnus "who both belong to the race of fairies and probably stem from Leda's eggs."

31. See C. G. Jung. "The Psychological Aspects of the Kore" in Jung and Kerényi. *Essays on a Science of Mythology.* Bollingen Series XXII. New York: Pantheon Press, 1949.

32. See Goethe's poem *"Der Fischer"* (The Fisher); Gottfried Keller's *"Nixie im Grundquell"* (Nixie in the Spring) (*Gesammelte Werke.* Berlin: W. Herz, 1891-92) and his *"Winternacht"* which is given in translation later in this article; Gerhart Hauptmann's *The Sunken Bell* (Freely rendered into English by C. H. Meltzer. Garden City, N.Y.: Doubleday Page & Co., 1914); Jean Giraudoux's *Undine* (English version prepared in conjunction with Schuyler Watts. New York, 1941).

33. *Minne* meaning love. Cf. *Minnesänger* (Singer of Love). See W. Grimm. *Deutsche Mythologie, l. c.,* Vol. I, p. 360. According to F. Kluge in *Deutsches Mythologisches Wörterbuch* the original meaning of the word *Minne* is remembrance, commemoration, recollection. It is related to the English word mind, and stems from the Indo-Germanic root *men* or *man,* meaning thinking, meaning. Grimm connects it with *manus, man.*

34. See, for example, the interesting study by R. Bezzola on *"Guillaume IX de Poitiers"* in *Romania,* Vol. LXVI.

35. John Rhys. *Celtic Folklore.* Oxford: Clarendon Press, 1901. p. 3 ff.

36. To iron is attributed the power of protecting against elfin beings.

37. This is quite startlingly described in a northern fairy tale *"Die Waldfrau"* (The Forest Woman) (*Märchen der Weltliteratur, l. c.*) which tells of a wood-chopper, enchanted by a beautiful maiden whom he has met in the forest. Every night she takes him with her into her mountain where everything is more splendid than anything he has ever seen. One day, as he is chopping, she brings him a meal in a beautiful silver bowl but, as she sits down on the tree trunk, he sees — to his horror — that she has a cow's tail and that it has fallen into the cleft in the tree. Quickly, he pulls out his wedge so that the tail is caught and pinched off. Then he writes the name of Jesus on the bowl. Immediately the woman disappears, and the bowl with the food becomes nothing but a piece of beef with cow dung on it.

38. The mirror is known in folk superstition as an instrument of magic. It has a numinous effect, since one sees one's shadow or double in it. A magic mirror shows what is happening all over the world, or it foretells the future and in general reveals secret and hidden things.

(See *Handwörterbuch des Deutschen Aberglaubens. l. c.,* Vol. IX under *"Spiegel"*).

39. See C. G. Jung. *Paracelsica* (Zürich: Rascher Verlag, 1942) where the legend is fully told, and the figure of Melusine is interpreted as the anima in connection with alchemical symbolism and the Paracelsian concept of the Melusines as dwelling in the blood.
40. From S. Baring-Gould. *Curious Myths of the Middle Ages.* London, Oxford & Cambridge: Rivingtons, 1869.
41. As, for instance, Lourdes.
42. After Alfred Maury. *Croyances et Légendes du Moyen-Age.* Paris: 1896.
43. *William Sharp (Fiona Macleod):* A Memoir compiled by his wife Elizabeth Sharp. New York: Duffield & Co., 1912, p. 9.
44. *Ibid.,* p. 9.
45. English version by the translator. (Ed. note)
46. *Four Treatises of Theophrastus von Hohenheim, called Paracelsus.* Edited by Sigerist. Baltimore: John Hopkins Press, 1941. p. 236.
47. *Ibid.,* p. 239 ff.
48. F. de la Motte Fouqué. *Undine.* Translated from the German by Edmund Gosse. London: Sidgwick & Jackson, Ltd., 1912.
49. Carl Gustav Carus. *Psyche.* Jena: Diederichs Verlag, 1926.
50. The loss of Berthalda's necklace having been brought about by Undine's water guardians, without her foreknowledge. (Ed. note)
51. That this same material has been used very recently by Giraudoux in his play *Undine* shows that it is not yet outdated.
52. *Four Lais of Marie de France — Guingamor, Lanval, Tydet, Bisclavet.* Rendered into English by Jessie L. Weston. London: D. Nutt, 1910.
53. A similar German legend is reported by Paracelsus in the treatise mentioned above, as also in W. Grimm in *Deutsche Sagen.* (Munich & Leipzig: Georg Mueller, No date. Vol. II) It tells of a knight from Stauffenberg who, one day as he was riding to church, met a marvelously beautiful maiden sitting all alone at the edge of a forest. As it turned out, she had been waiting there for him. She told him that she had always loved and guarded him, whereupon they became engaged. This maiden, too, was a fairy who could always be summoned by wishing. She provided him with money and property on the condition that he should form no tie with another woman. When his family pressed him to marry and he agreed to do so in spite of this, she first gave him a warning, then brought about his death mysteriously within three days. In this maiden who has loved the knight *since the beginning,* it is not difficult to recognize his own feminine element; its exclusive demand is a characteristic anima trait which often leads to difficult conflicts and entanglements.
54. See J. A. MacCullough. *The Religion of the Ancient Celts. l. c.*

55. This motif plays an important role in, for example, Chrétien de Troyes' poems *"Yvain"* and *"Erec and Enide."* The last work is the subject of a very discriminating study by R. Bezzola (*Le sens de l'Adventure et de l'Amour.* Paris: Ed. La jeune Parque). The heaviest task of the lovelorn hero consists in his having to fight with an opponent in the same condition, that is, to some extent with his double. Overcoming him signifies that he can liberate himself from the isolating enchantment of love and turn back with his wife to society and the world.

56. P. S. Barto. *Tannhäuser and the Mountain of Venus.* New York: Oxford University Press, American branch, 1916. See pp. 74, 75 for the English version given here which precisely parallels the German given by Mrs. Jung. (Ed. note)

57. In some versions it says *"Venus der Düvelinne"* (Venus of the Devilesses).

58. Here Venus has become the Swiss Verena.

59. Unfortunately no English rendering of this could be found. It runs roughly:

> "Danuser was a wondrous youth
> Great wonders came he to see.
> He came to Lady Venere's mount
> To those beauteous maidens three.

> "Throughout the week they're fair all day
> Decked out with silk and gold,
> Rings and beads and crowns of May,
> But Sunday they're otters and snakes."

60. Barto. *l. c.,* p. 95. The version given by Mrs. Jung runs as follows:

> *"Do was er wider in den Berg*
> *Und het sin lieb erkoren.*
> *Des must der vierte Babst Urban*
> *Auch ewiglich sein verloren."*

61. See also W. Grimm. *Deutsche Mythologie. l. c.* In the later Middle Ages in Germany, Venusberg was identified with the Grail, this appellation in the course of time having acquired the meaning of feast and merriment. W. Hertz quotes a chronicler who says: "History writers believe that the swan knight came from the mountain where Venus is in the Grail." *(Parzival und der Graal)*

62. For a detailed psychological study of this work, see Linda Fierz-David: *The Dream of Poliphilo.* Bollingen Series XXV. New York: Pantheon Press, 1950.

63. Antoine de la Sale. *Le Paradis de la Sibylle.* Edited and with a critical commentary by Fernand Desonay. Paris: Librairie E. Droz, 1930.

64. See W. J. Roscher. *Lexikon der griechischen und römischen Mythologie.*

65. *Le Paradis de la Sibylle. l. c.*
66. *Ibid.*
67. The image of the goddess, a sacred stone, was at that time taken from Pessinus and brought to Rome.
68. In an Orphic hymn she is invoked as "Preserver of Life and Friend of raging Passion." *(Orpheus, Altgriechische Mysteriengesänge.* Translated into German by J. O. Plassmann. Jena: Dietrichs Verlag, 1928)
69. One could also designate it as the "realm of the Mothers" (Goethe). I chose the other term because in this story it is not the maternal aspect of the feminine, but the eros aspect, that stands foremost.
70. K. Kerényi. *"Die Göttin Natur"* in *Eranos-Jahrbuch* XIV. Zürich: Rhein-Verlag, 1947.
71. C. G. Jung. *Symbole der Wandlung.* 4th edit. Zürich: Rascher Verlag, 1952. p. 513 & p. 610. For English, see *Psychology of the Unconscious.* New York: Moffat Yard & Co., 1921. p. 183 & p. 211. (Will be Vol. V in the *Collected Works*)
72. See C. G. Jung, *ibid.;* also Erich Neumann. *The Origin and History of Consciousness.* Bollingen Series XLII. New York: Pantheon Press, 1954.
73. Jung and Kerényi. *Essays on a Science of Mythology. l. c.,* p. 242.
74. I refer you to Aniela Jaffé's excellent study, *Bilder und Symbols aus E. T. A. Hoffmanns Märchen "Der goldne Topf,"* included in C. G. Jung's *Gestaltungen des Unbewussten.* Zürich: Rascher Verlag, 1950.
75. Pierre Benoit. *Atlantida.* Translated into English by Mary C. Tongue and Mary Ross. New York: Duffield & Co., 1920.
76. Jung and Kerenyi. *Essays on a Science of Mythology. l. c.,* "The Psychological Aspects of the Kore," p. 241.
77. C. G. Jung. *Symbole der Wandlung. l. c.* (for English, see note 71); and E. Neumann. *The Origin and History of Consciousness. l. c.*
78. See C. G. Jung. *"Uber die Archetypen des kollectiven Unbewussten"* in *Von dem Wurzeln des Bewusstseins.* An English translation of this revised article will be published in Vol. X of the *Collected Works.* At present the only English version available is the unrevised article entitled "Archetypes of the Collective Unconscious" in *Integration of the Personality.* New York: Farrar & Rinehart, Inc., 1939. For reference to the anima, see p. 77; to the Wise Man, p. 88. See also Jung's "The Phenomenology of the Spirit in Fairy Tales" in *Spirit and Nature.* Bollingen Series XXX.1. New York: Pantheon Press, 1954.
79. Quoted by C. G. Jung in "The Spirit of Psychology" in *Nature and Spirit. l. c.,* pp. 405, 406. See also *Paracelsus Selected Writings.* Bollingen Series XXVIII. New York: Pantheon Press, 1951. p. 255.
80. C. G. Jung. "The Relations Between the Ego and the Unconscious" in *Two Essays on Analytical Psychology.* Bollingen Series XX. New York: Pantheon Press, 1953.

81. Jung and Kerényi. *Essays on a Science of Mythology. l. c.,* p. 228 ff.
82. J. K. Musaeus. *Volksmärchen der Deutschen,* Vol. II, in *Märchen der Weltliteratur. l. c.*
83. The story also describes the fates of the couple's three daughters, which I will not go into here.
84. *William Sharp (Fiona Macleod):* A Memoir compiled by his wife Elizabeth Sharp, *l. c.*
85. *Ibid.,* p. 227.
86. *Ibid.,* p. 285.
87. See Linda Fierz-David. *The Dream of Poliphilo. l. c.,* p. 210.

Published by Spring Publications

Adolf Guggenbühl-Craig   *MARRIAGE—DEAD OR ALIVE*

In a series of fast-moving, trenchant chapters, this leading Jungian psychiatrist examines marriage against the background of individuation, thereby radicalizing our conventional notions. Divorce and children, perversions and affairs, sacrifice and individualism—these are only some of the emotional issues that Dr. Guggenbühl attacks with his customary vigor and deceptively facile style. Translated by Murray Stein. 126 pages.

Adolf Guggenbühl-Craig   *EROS ON CRUTCHES*

Guggenbühl-Craig takes up the frightening decay in morality that allows psychopathy to live close by without recognition. Today we can hardly see the psychopath, or our own psychopathic traits. Guggenbühl evokes sympathy for this figure even as he explores his defects of character. In the psychopath's soul Eros is on crutches. An important contribution to precise diagnostics for the clinician and to reflection on evil and compassion. 126 pages.

James Hillman   *INSEARCH:PSYCHOLOGY AND RELIGION*

Widely used in pastoral counseling and psychotherapeutic training. Sets out the fundamental principles and attitudes of Jungian psychology in a simple, yet deeply experiential style. "Probably Hillman's most humanly feeling book . . . recommended for dream interpretation and practical examples." Although translated into Dutch, German, Japanese and Italian, the original edition had been out of print for years. 126 pages.

James Hillman   *SUICIDE AND THE SOUL*

A classic introduction to the experience of depth psychology. A treatise on death and suicide that explores with a polemical passion the differences between a medical model of therapy and one that engages the soul. 192 pages.

P.O.Box 222069 Dallas, Texas 75222